Life Skills Playbook for Teen Boys

How to Navigate Challenges, Gain Practical Skills, and Build Confidence So You Can Thrive at Life

Alex and Riley Harper

Copyright © 2024 by Alex and Riley Harper

All rights reserved.

No portion of this book may be reproduced in any form without written permission from the publisher or author, except as permitted by U.S. copyright law.

This publication is designed to provide accurate and authoritative information in regard to the subject matter covered. It is sold with the understanding that neither the author nor the publisher is engaged in rendering legal, investment, accounting or other professional services. While the publisher and author have used their best efforts in preparing this book, they make no representations or warranties with respect to the accuracy or completeness of the contents of this book and specifically disclaim any implied warranties of merchantability or fitness for a particular purpose. No warranty may be created or extended by sales representatives or written sales materials. The advice and strategies contained herein may not be suitable for your situation. You should consult with a professional when appropriate. Neither the publisher nor the author shall be liable for any loss of profit or any other commercial damages, including but not limited to special, incidental, consequential, personal, or other damages.

First edition 2024

Contents

Introduction 1
  Empowering Teen Boys: Addressing the Skills Gap 1
    The Reality of Teenage Struggles................................... 2
    Consequences of Skill Deficiency 6
    A Path Forward: Building Confident and Capable Young Men 9

Chapter 1: Building Confidence and Self-Esteem 12
  Building Confidence and Self-Esteem 12
    Self-Affirmation Exercises to Boost Self-Esteem and Self-Confidence 13
    Overcoming Self-Doubt and Imposter Syndrome 17
    Setting Achievable Goals and Celebrating Successes..... 21
    Effective Communication Skills for Asserting Oneself... 24

Chapter 2: Health and Wellness Habits 28
  Leading a Healthy and Balanced Lifestyle 28
    The Importance of Regular Exercise.............................. 29
    Healthy Eating Habits 33
    Developing a Positive Body Image 40

Chapter 3: Practical Skills for Daily Life......................... 45
  Essential Practical Skills... 45
    Basic Auto Mechanics and Maintenance....................... 46
  Essential Home Repair and DIY Skills 51
  Understanding Basic Tools for Household Repairs 51
    Getting Familiar with Essential Tools............................. 51
    The Multi-Purpose Hammer... 51
    Unraveling the Mystery of Screwdrivers........................ 51
    The Handy Pliers 52
    Mastering the Wrench... 52

Fixing a Loose Cabinet Door..56
Fixing a Leaky Faucet... 57
Putting It Into Action 59
Financial Literacy and Money Management 60

Chapter 4: Time Management and Productivity Tips.............65
Effective Time Management 65
Creating a Daily Schedule and Prioritizing Tasks for Maximum Productivity..66
Avoiding Procrastination and Staying Focused on Goals..........70
Utilizing Technology Tools for Better Time Management and Organization 74
    The Power of Productivity Apps... 74
    Time-Tracking for the Win... 76
    Task Automation Magic... 77
Balancing Schoolwork, Extracurricular Activities, and Personal Time Efficiently 78

Chapter 5: Effective Communication Skills 84
Enhancing Communication Skills in Teenage Boys 84
    Improving Understanding and Empathy through Active Listening.. 85
    Developing Clear and Respectful Communication through Assertiveness Training.. 90
    Handling Disputes Positively through Conflict Resolution Techniques.. 97

Chapter 6: Decision Making and Problem-Solving Skills 100
Critical Thinking and Problem-Solving Skills.........................100
Analyzing Situations for Thoughtful Decision-Making 101
Equipping with Problem- Solving Techniques 105
Seeking Guidance and Support..114

iv

Chapter 7: Understanding and Managing Emotions ... 119
Enhancing Emotional Awareness ... 120
Managing Stress and Anxiety ... 123
Healthy Coping Mechanisms ... 127
Mindfulness Practices ... 132

Chapter 8: Healthy Relationships and Boundaries ... 137
Identifying Toxic Relationships and Developing Boundaries . 138
Respecting Personal Boundaries and
Ensuring Mutual Respect ... 142
Effective Ways to Communicate Boundaries
and Assert Personal Space ... 146
Building Positive Peer Relationships Based on Trust and
Support ... 150

Chapter 9: Coping with Challenges and Adversity ... 155
Developing a Growth Mindset ... 156
Coping Strategies for Stress and Anxiety ... 160
Seeking Support During Adversity ... 164
Turning Challenges into Opportunities ... 168

Chapter 10: Planning for the Future- Career and Education 174
Exploring Career Paths and Interests ... 175
Preparing for College or Vocational Training ... 179
Setting Academic Goals and Developing a Study Plan ... 183
    Establish SMART Goals ... 183
    Create a Study Schedule ... 184
    Seek Academic Support ... 185
    Monitor Progress Regularly ... 186
Developing Networking Skills and Building Professional
Relationships ... 188

Looking Forward with Confidence 191

References 193

Don't Forget to Claim Your FREE Bonus Chapters…

-Cooking Basics
-Resume and Interview Tips

Scan Here!

Introduction

Empowering Teen Boys: Addressing the Skills Gap

Picture that it's a bright, sunny afternoon, and you just got the keys to your first car—a hand-me-down, but still pretty cool. You're cruising down the road, feeling invincible, when suddenly, BAM! A flat tire strikes. You're stranded, scratching your head, wondering if calling for help or Googling "how to change a tire" is the way to go. Ever been there? If not, trust me, you don't want to be. But here's the kicker—what if I told you this scenario happens every day because many teenage boys aren't equipped with some basic, yet crucial, practical skills?

Let's dive deeper. Take Mike, for example, a 16-year-old who found himself clueless on the side of the road, staring at that deflated tire like it was an alien artifact. His story isn't unique. Or consider Josh, neck-deep in schoolwork and part-time jobs, struggling to manage time and emotions, constantly feeling like he's juggling flaming torches without any training. And then there's Billy, who blew his first paycheck before realizing rent was due, simply because personal finance was as foreign to him as ancient Greek. These aren't isolated incidents— they're symptoms of a larger issue where essential life and emotional skills are left in the shadows of traditional academic education.

So, what gives? In this book, we're diving into how to bridge that gap—empowering you with abilities that extend beyond textbooks and exams. From mastering the art of simple car maintenance, cooking a meal that won't send anyone running, and understanding how to make your money last, to navigating the emotional ups and downs of teenage life, we've got it covered. Buckle up, because by the end of this read, you'll be more prepared to tackle those real-world challenges and maybe even help someone else along the way.

The Reality of Teenage Struggles

Picture this: Mike, a 16-year-old high school sophomore, is driving home from his part-time job at the local grocery store. Suddenly, he hears a concerning thump-thump-thump sound coming from his car. Pulling over to the side of the road, he steps out and finds that he has a flat tire. After a few moments of staring blankly at the deflated rubber, Mike realizes he has absolutely no idea how to change it. Frustrated, he calls his dad, who drives over to help him out.

Mike's situation isn't unique. In fact, it's quite common. According to UNICEF, nearly three- quarters of young people aged 15 to 24 lack the necessary skills for employment (UNICEF, n.d.). If we dig deeper, it's apparent that this gap isn't limited to just job-specific skills. Many teenagers today also struggle with basic practical life skills that are crucial for daily living.

Think about it—changing a flat tire, managing an allowance, cooking a simple meal, handling stressors effectively—these are the kinds of skills that can make or break your day-to-day experience. Yet, there's a glaring deficiency in these essential abilities among teenage boys. The reason? It often boils down to educational systems placing a higher emphasis on academic achievement rather than on holistic life skills training.

Teenage boys like Mike are facing a significant challenge. Without practical life skills and emotional intelligence, navigating daily hurdles becomes overwhelming, and confidence takes a hit. Research highlights the importance of addressing these issues head-on. For example, Beckman et al. (2021) found that adolescents express a vital need for stability and adult guidance to build lasting relationships and coping mechanisms. The absence of these elements leads to heightened stress and mental health challenges.

So, where do we start? First off, let's talk practical skills. These aren't reserved for survivalists or weekend hobbyists—they're everyday must-haves.

Imagine the sense of accomplishment and independence you'd feel by mastering these tasks:

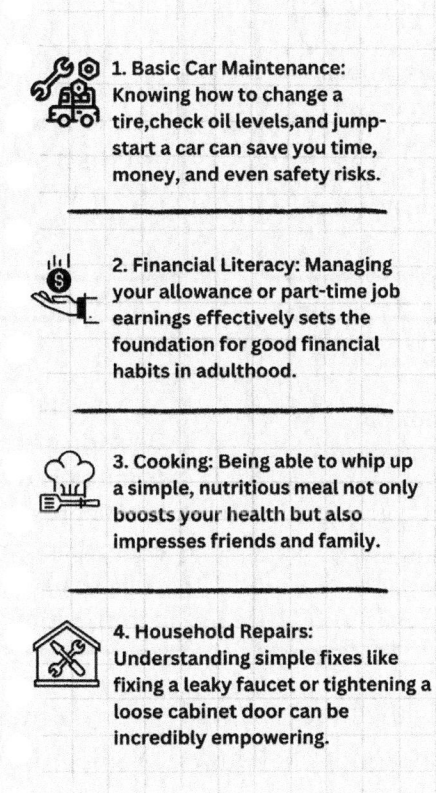

1. Basic Car Maintenance: Knowing how to change a tire, check oil levels, and jump-start a car can save you time, money, and even safety risks.

2. Financial Literacy: Managing your allowance or part-time job earnings effectively sets the foundation for good financial habits in adulthood.

3. Cooking: Being able to whip up a simple, nutritious meal not only boosts your health but also impresses friends and family.

4. Household Repairs: Understanding simple fixes like fixing a leaky faucet or tightening a loose cabinet door can be incredibly empowering.

Now, let's address a more subtle but equally important skill set: emotional intelligence. This includes being able to recognize, understand, and manage your emotions, as well as empathize with others. Emotional intelligence is often dubbed the "soft skill," yet it's fundamental. According to research by UNICEF, today's youth face significant barriers when seeking help for mental health issues due to stigmatizing attitudes and low availability of resources (Beckman et al., 2021). This makes it even more crucial to equip teens with emotional resilience tools.

Here's what you can do to bolster your emotional intelligence:

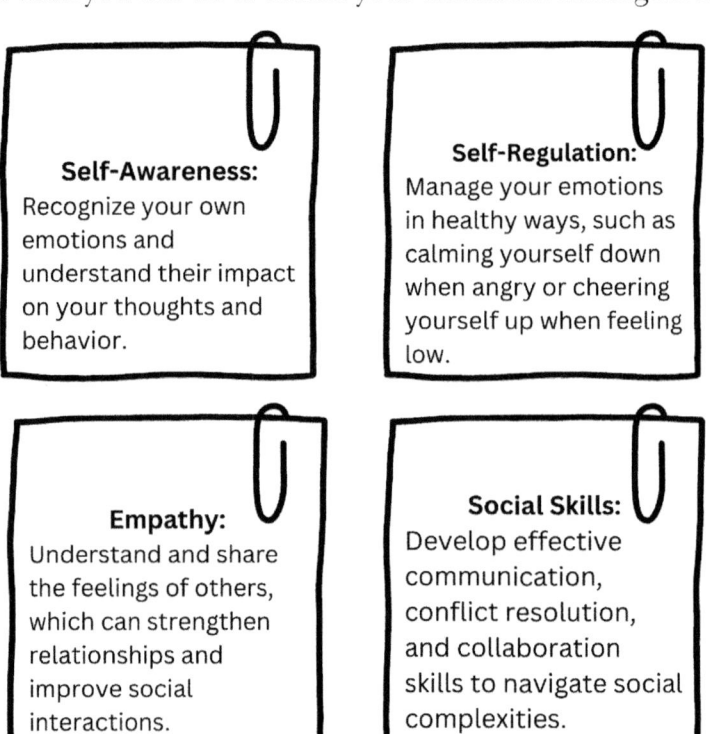

Equipping you with these essential skills ensures you are better prepared for real-world challenges. Remember, it's not about turning into a Renaissance man overnight. It's about gradually building a toolkit that complements academic knowledge and sets you up for lifelong success.

So, how does one go about gaining these skills? Fortunately, there are countless resources available. Schools can incorporate life skills training into the curriculum, offering workshops or elective courses that focus on both practical and emotional competencies. Community centers frequently offer classes on everything from basic car maintenance to emotional wellbeing.

Parents and guardians can play a pivotal role too. Simple activities like involving you in household chores, having open discussions about financial decisions, or practicing stress-relief techniques together can be enlightening. When you witness adults navigating life's challenges, you learn through observation and participation, developing those invaluable skills yourself.

Another innovative approach involves leveraging technology and online platforms. With countless tutorials and interactive courses readily available, learning a new skill has never been easier. Whether its YouTube videos on DIY home repairs or apps designed to improve emotional intelligence, you can access a wealth of information right from your smartphone!

Moreover, peer support groups can also be incredibly beneficial for you. Joining clubs or organizations where you can collaborate and learn from each other fosters a sense of community and shared growth. This can significantly enhance both practical skills and emotional wellbeing.

Let's give you the tools you need to not only survive but thrive. After all, when armed with the right skills, there's no flat tire,

financial conundrum, or emotional hurdle that you can't overcome. And who knows? Maybe next time Mike faces a flat tire, he won't just change it himself but might even help someone else along the way!

Consequences of Skill Deficiency

I remember meeting Jackson, a senior in high school who was drowning in stress. His story was filled with nights staring at textbooks that seemed to be written in hieroglyphics and weekends spent juggling part- time work and homework deadlines. One evening, after a particularly grueling day, Jackson confided in me about his struggle to manage his time and emotions. He felt like he was teetering on the edge of a cliff, with no safety net in sight.

Jackson's experience is far from unique. Many teen boys today are finding themselves ill-equipped to handle the myriad challenges life throws their way. While schools often do a great job teaching algebra and history, they sometimes gloss over the essential practical skills and emotional intelligence needed to navigate daily problems and build confidence. This oversight can leave you swirling in a vortex of confusion and anxiety, unsure how to untangle yourself from the demands of modern life.

Consider another example: Billy, fresh out of high school, received his first paycheck and decided to celebrate with friends. By the end of the month, he was scratching his head, trying to figure out why he couldn't afford rent. The problem? Personal finance wasn't a subject he'd mastered, or even scratched the surface of, during his school years. And let's not forget Sam, whose academic stress turned into crippling self-doubt because he didn't know how to cope with failure or ask for help constructively.

These stories highlight the stark reality: without proper guidance and skills, many of you face significant hurdles. Empirical research supports this notion. For instance, studies have shown that life skills training can profoundly affect long-term outcomes for teens, particularly those at high risk (Campbell-Heider et al., 2009). Programs aimed at developing personal finance management, communication, and problem-solving skills have proven effective in reducing mental health issues and substance use among adolescents.

Let's tackle these common struggles head-on. Academic pressures weigh heavily on you, leading to stress and anxiety. Peer pressure adds another layer of complexity, pushing you toward behaviors you might otherwise avoid. And then there's the looming uncertainty about the future—college, careers, relationships—each decision feeling monumental and final. It's no wonder many feel overwhelmed.

Supporting you in developing these skills isn't just about preventing negative outcomes; it's about empowering you to thrive. Research underscores this point. According to JumpIn Northwest, the absence of basic life skills, such as effective communication, problem-solving, and personal finance management is leaving a generation unprepared for the real world

(Anderson, 2023). Programs focusing on teaching these skills in a structured manner can offer you the confidence and competence you need to succeed.

One critical area we need to focus on is communication skills. Boys often grapple with expressing their emotions, partly due to societal expectations to "man up" and partly because you're not taught how to articulate your feelings. Learning how to use open dialogue and active listening can significantly enhance your interpersonal relationships. When you learn to communicate effectively, you can resolve conflicts amicably, collaborate better in team settings, and build stronger bonds with peers and family members.

Learning how to manage personal finances is another game-changer. Simple practices like budgeting, understanding interest rates, savings, and basic investment principles can provide you with a sense of control over your financial futures. This knowledge alleviates the stress associated with money management and lays a foundation for responsible financial behavior in adulthood.

Moreover, equipping you with problem-solving abilities fosters independence and resilience. Life inevitably throws curveballs, and having the skills to analyze situations, weigh options, and make informed decisions can turn potential crises into manageable challenges. This empowerment reduces anxiety and

builds self-efficacy, enabling you to approach the future with a balanced perspective.

Emphasizing emotional intelligence is equally important. Learning to recognize, understand, and manage your emotions helps prevent mental health issues and promotes overall well-being. Activities like mindfulness meditation, journaling, and even role- playing scenarios can be integrated into your routines to develop these competencies.

To achieve this goal:

- Keep a journal to reflect on your experiences and track your emotional responses.
- Use mindfulness practices through apps or group sessions to help you stay grounded and present.
- Find safe spaces where you feel comfortable discussing your feelings and challenges without fear of judgment.

Another vital aspect is fostering a growth mindset. You should understand that intelligence and abilities aren't fixed traits but can be developed through effort and perseverance. Highlighting examples of famous personalities who overcame failures to achieve success can inspire you to embrace challenges and view setbacks as opportunities for growth.

A Path Forward: Building Confident and Capable Young Men

So, let's take a step back and remember what we've talked about so far. We kicked things off with Mike, the kid who got stuck by the side of the road because he didn't know how to change a tire. This isn't just about flat tires; it's about being prepared for life's hiccups—big and small.

And then there was Josh, practically swimming in stress, feeling like life was one giant pop quiz with no answer sheet in sight. His story is a wake-up call that a lot of teenage guys might be missing some crucial skills. Schools are great at cramming our brains with facts and figures but sometimes drop the ball when it comes to teaching practical stuff. We're talking everything from managing money to managing emotions.

The reality? If you don't know these basic skills, life can feel like trying to juggle flaming swords—just without any circus applause. And that can lead to all sorts of trouble, from financial woes to emotional burnout. Research even backs this up. Studies show that teens equipped with life skills tend to dodge a slew of problems later on (Campbell-Heider et al., 2009).

But hey, don't start panicking yet. The good news is, these skills can be learned. Picture this: You, mastering not just one skill, but a whole toolkit of them. Imagine knowing how to cook a meal that doesn't come from a microwave, or how to talk about your feelings without sounding like you're auditioning for a soap opera. Think of the confidence boost when you realize you can handle whatever life throws your way.

Now, before you roll your eyes and think this sounds like homework, hear me out. It's actually pretty cool stuff. Start small. Ask your parents to show you how to change a tire or unclog a drain. Try some basic budgeting with your allowance. Download an app to learn a new skill, whether it's cooking or coding. And for the love of pizza, don't bottle up your feelings; find someone to talk to, even if it's just writing in a journal.

Looking at the bigger picture, it's not just about surviving high school. It's about setting yourself up for success beyond graduation. When you're equipped with these practical and emotional skills, you're not just ready to face the challenges—you're ready to crush them. Plus, these skills make life a whole lot easier. Who knows? Maybe you'll be the guy who helps out a stranded friend with a flat tire one day.

> In short, gaining these essential skills isn't just about dodging pitfalls. It's about paving the way for a smoother ride through life. So, next time life throws you a curveball, you'll be able to catch it —and maybe even throw it back with a smile.

CHAPTER 1

Building Confidence and Self-Esteem

Building Confidence and Self-Esteem

Imagine you're trying to climb a mountain, but instead of using the proper gear, you've strapped toaster ovens to your feet. Sounds ridiculous, right? Yet, that's exactly what it feels like going through life without confidence—clumsy, ill-equipped, and much harder than it needs to be. Confidence isn't just some magic trait only a few lucky people are born with. It's something everyone can build, including teenage boys. With a bit of focus, some humor, and the right exercises, you'll find that tackling life's challenges becomes less like climbing a mountain barefoot and more like a well-planned adventure.

Confidence, or the lack thereof, is a universal issue, but it's particularly tricky during the teenage years. Imagine standing in front of your class for a presentation on World War II, knees shaking like they've got their own jazz rhythm section. Or how about asking your crush to go to the movies and finding your throat drier than the Sahara Desert? These moments of self-doubt can feel overwhelming, making simple tasks seem impossible. You know you have the potential—you've got the brains and the skills—but that nagging voice in your head keeps saying you're not good enough. It's like having an annoying backseat driver on the road trip of your life.

In this chapter, we'll dig into techniques to build the kind of confidence that helps you navigate these teenage years with resilience and determination. We'll cover self-affirmation exercises that are as easy to add to your routine as brushing your teeth (minus the minty freshness). You'll learn how to flip your self-talk from harsh critique to enthusiastic coach and how visualization can turn your dreams into achievable goals. Plus, we'll show you how to tap into your unique talents and celebrate those small victories that lead to big wins. By the time you're done, you'll have a toolkit packed with strategies to boost your self-esteem and face life's challenges with a confident stride. So let's toss those metaphorical toaster ovens aside and get started on this journey to a stronger, more assured you!

Self-Affirmation Exercises to Boost Self-Esteem and Self-Confidence

One of the most powerful tools teenage boys can use to tackle life's challenges is confidence. Confidence doesn't just appear out of thin air; it's something you build, like muscle in the gym. And let's face it, while hitting the weights might get those biceps bulging, working on your self-confidence will make facing life's hurdles a breeze. So, where do we start? Self- affirmation exercises.

First up, practicing daily affirmations. Think of affirmations as the mental equivalent of brushing your teeth—something simple you do every day to keep things in check. By repeating positive statements about yourself, you can rewire negative thought patterns and build a positive self-image. Sounds like magic, right? Well, it's actually science (Affirmations For Self-Esteem And Why They Work, n.d.). The brain's reward system gets activated when you say nice things about yourself, creating new neural pathways that replace old, negative ones.

Here's how you can kickstart this:

 Start by writing down a few positive statements about yourself. These could be about your abilities, qualities, or anything you take pride in.

 Every morning, stand in front of the mirror, look yourself in the eye, and repeat these statements.

 Do this before bedtime as well. Consistency is key here—think of it as feeding your brain a steady diet of positivity.

Once you've got those affirmations flowing, let's talk self-talk. No, not the kind where you're debating that epic game strategy with your buddies, but the internal dialogue you have with yourself. Focusing this self-talk on your strengths and achievements can seriously boost your confidence and self-esteem. Rather than dwelling on what went wrong, remind yourself of times when you nailed it. For instance, if you rocked that history presentation, tell yourself: "I'm great at presenting and explaining complex topics."

To maintain this empowering inner chatter, you can:

- Keep a journal where you jot down small victories each day. It could be anything from acing a test to helping a friend.
- Whenever self-doubt creeps in, flip through your journal and remind yourself of all the cool stuff you've accomplished.

Now, let's add another tool to our confidence- building toolkit: visualization. Visualizing successful outcomes can increase self-belief and confidence. Athletes use this technique all the time—imagine scoring that winning goal or giving a flawless performance before it even happens. Surprisingly, your brain often can't tell the difference between a real event and a vividly imagined one (Cascio et al., 2016). Here's how you can make this work for you:

- Find a quiet place where you won't be disturbed, close your eyes, and take a few deep breaths.
- Picture yourself achieving your goals in detail. Imagine the sights, sounds, and even the emotions you'll feel.
- Mentally rehearse the steps you'll take to get there. This way, when the actual moment arrives, it won't feel entirely new or intimidating.

Now, onto showcasing your talents and skills. Engaging in activities that let you flex your unique abilities can reinforce a sense of self-worth. Whether it's playing an instrument, participating in sports, or even mastering video games, every skill you hone adds to your confidence bank. Here's a way to go about this:

- Identify activities that you enjoy and are good at—this is your zone of genius.
- Commit to spending regular time on these activities. Join clubs, participate in competitions, or simply practice consistently.
- Share your progress with friends and family. Their encouragement can be incredibly uplifting and further reinforce your belief in yourself.

But wait, why stop there? We all know consistency is vital. The consistent practice of these self-affirmation exercises leads to improved self-esteem and confidence levels. It's like training for a marathon; you wouldn't just run once and expect to ace it. You train regularly, building endurance and strength over time. In the same way, make these exercises a part of your daily routine.

Another thing to remember is that building confidence is a journey, not a destination. There will be ups and downs, but that's perfectly okay. What's important is that you stay committed to the process. Just like a gamer leveling up, each positive step you take moves you closer to becoming the best version of yourself.

So, whether you're facing exams, social challenges, or planning the next big move in your life, these self-affirmation exercises can arm you with the confidence needed to tackle anything head-on. Remember, the world is your oyster, and with a confident stride, you'll open up countless opportunities.

By making these practices a habit, you'll find that you're not only building a stronger sense of self but also inspiring others around you. After all, confidence is contagious. When you shine brightly, you encourage others to light up, too. And who knows? That positive energy might just create a ripple effect, sparking change far beyond what you ever imagined.

In summary, setting aside a few minutes each day for affirmations, redirecting self-talk towards strengths, visualizing success, and engaging in activities that showcase your talents can collectively bolster your confidence. The road to becoming a more assured you might be long, but it's undoubtedly worth every step. So, lace up those mental sneakers and embark on this transformative journey with determination and a smile. You've got this!

Overcoming Self-Doubt and Imposter Syndrome

Building confidence can be a game-changer for teenage boys, helping them navigate life's obstacles with resilience and determination. One of the biggest hurdles to developing this crucial trait is overcoming self-doubt and the ever-pesky imposter syndrome. Let's dive into how to tackle these internal battles head-on.

First things first, let's talk about identifying and challenging negative self-beliefs. Imagine you're walking around with a backpack stuffed full of homework assignments that you don't need to carry anymore. That's pretty much what negative self- beliefs are like—they weigh you down unnecessarily. The good news? You can start unpacking this metaphorical backpack. Here's how:

- **Recognize those limiting thoughts:** Pay attention when your inner critic gets loud. If you catch yourself thinking, "I can't do this" or "I'm not good enough," make a mental note of it.

- **Question their validity:** Ask yourself, "Is this really true?" Most often, you'll find these thoughts have little basis in reality.
- **Replace them with positives:** Swap out "I can't" with "I can learn" or "I'm working on it." Over time, you'll notice a shift in how you perceive challenges.

Remember, feelings of inadequacy are often based on unfounded fears rather than facts (Feder, 2023).

Next up on our checklist is seeking feedback and constructive criticism. Now, I know what you're thinking—"Who voluntarily asks for criticism?" But hear me out. Getting feedback is like having a roadmap. It shows you where you're doing well and where you might need a bit more practice:

- **Talk to trusted peers and mentors:** These people have your best interests at heart and can provide genuine insights.
- **Be open and receptive:** Remember, feedback isn't an attack. It's an opportunity to grow.
- **Apply the feedback:** Use it to fine-tune your skills and approach. This will give you a clearer picture of your strengths and areas for improvement.

Constructive criticism might sting a little, but don't let it deter you. It's all part of the process of becoming a better version of yourself (Cleveland Clinic, n.d.).

Setting realistic expectations and understanding that mistakes are part of the learning process comes next. Often, we set the bar way too high for ourselves.

We aim to be perfect, which sets us up for disappointment. Instead, try to:

- **Set achievable goals:** Break down big tasks into smaller, more manageable steps.
- **Embrace mistakes:** Treat them as lessons rather than failures. Missed a shot during a game? Analyze what went wrong and adjust.
- **Celebrate small wins:** Every step forward is progress. Give yourself credit for the effort and improvements you make along the way.

We've all stumbled while trying to master something new. Think about learning to ride a bike—falling is practically a rite of passage. Just remember, every misstep is a stepping stone.

Another key concept is cultivating a growth mindset. This is all about focusing on continuous improvement and learning from failures instead of being bogged down by them.

Here's how to adopt this winning mindset:

- **View challenges as opportunities:** Every obstacle is a chance to learn something new. Instead of shying away, dive in and see what you can gain from the experience.
- **Stay curious:** Always look for ways to expand your skills and knowledge. Whether it's reading a book, watching a tutorial, or asking questions, keep that thirst for learning alive.
- **Reflect on your progress:** Take time to look back at how far you've come. Journaling can be a great tool for this. Write about your accomplishments, however small they may seem.

When you believe you can improve through effort and perseverance, setbacks become less daunting and more like temporary hurdles.

Let's not forget the importance of addressing self-doubt directly to pave the way for increased self-confidence and resilience. It's crucial to realize that everyone deals with self-doubt at some point. The trick is not to let it stall your growth.

Think of self-doubt as a noisy neighbor who keeps playing loud music. You can either let it disturb your peace or choose to ignore it and focus on your own melody. By consistently practicing these strategies, you'll build a reliable toolkit to shut down doubt whenever it arises.

So, let's recap the road map:

- **Identify and challenge negative self-beliefs:** Recognize them, question them, replace them.
- **Seek feedback and constructive criticism:** Find trusted sources, stay open, apply what you learn.
- **Set realistic expectations:** Aim for incremental progress, celebrate small victories, and view mistakes as part of the journey.
- **Cultivate a growth mindset:** Embrace challenges, stay curious, and reflect on your progress.

It's all about more action and less fretting over perfection. Confidence isn't an overnight delivery; it's built gradually, brick by brick. So, go easy on yourself, keep pushing forward, and before you know it, you'll handle life's curveballs like a pro. After all, even superheroes had to start somewhere!

Setting Achievable Goals and Celebrating Successes

Let's talk about confidence, especially for teenage boys. Confidence is not just a nice-to-have trait; it's the fuel that keeps the engine running when things get tough. And let's face it, teenage years can be like a roller coaster ride—thrilling, terrifying, and often confusing. But with a little focus on setting achievable goals and celebrating successes, we can make this wild ride a bit more manageable and enjoyable.

First things first, breaking down larger goals into smaller, manageable tasks. Imagine you're faced with this gigantic mountain, and your task is to climb it.

Sounds daunting, right? But if you take it step by step, suddenly it's just a series of hills.

Here's what you can do to break down those big, scary goals:

- **Start by identifying the end goal.** What is it you want to achieve? Let's say, for example, you want to improve at basketball. That's your mountain.
- **Break that down into smaller, actionable tasks.** Maybe start with dribbling practice for 15 minutes a day. Once you're comfortable dribbling, move on to shooting from different spots on the court.
- **Keep track of your progress.** Use a notebook or an app to mark off each task as you complete it. This way, you can see how far you've come and what still needs to be done.

Trust me, every time you tick off one of these smaller tasks, you'll feel a little surge of confidence. It's like getting better at a sport—each small achievement brings you closer to mastering the whole game. (Health & Wellness Services, 2024).

Now, let's talk about recognizing and celebrating milestones. No matter how small, achievements should be celebrated. Think of it as giving yourself a high-five every time you hit a mini milestone on your way to the big goal. It's these little 'wins' that keep the momentum going.

Here's a simple guide to help you celebrate these victories:

- **Make a list of all the mini-milestones** within your bigger goal. For instance, if your main goal is to improve in math, celebrate when you ace a test or finally understand a tricky concept.
- **Plan small rewards** for each milestone achieved. It could be something as simple as allowing yourself an extra 30 minutes of video game time or treating yourself to your favorite snack.
- **Share your successes with others.** Tell your friends, family, or mentors about your progress. Their encouragement will amplify your own sense of accomplishment.

Recognizing and celebrating these small steps helps reinforce a sense of accomplishment, boosting your overall confidence (Action for Happiness, n.d.).

Of course, not everything will go smoothly. Setbacks are part of any journey, but they don't have to derail you. Learning from setbacks can actually enhance your resilience and motivation.

When you hit a bump in the road, here's how you can turn it into a learning opportunity:

- **Acknowledge the setback.** Pretending it didn't happen doesn't help anyone. Own it and analyze what went wrong.
- **Adjust your goals accordingly.** Maybe you aimed too high too soon. Scale back a bit, and set a more attainable target.
- **Stay flexible.** Sometimes the path you initially chose isn't the best one. Be willing to change your approach if needed.

Think of setbacks as unexpected plot twists in your hero's journey. They add depth to your story and make the eventual success even sweeter (lparsons, 2024).

Lastly, no hero embarks on their journey alone. Establishing a support system is crucial. We all need people who can cheer us on, offer advice, and hold us accountable.

Here's how you can build your own squad of supporters:

- **Identify who in your life can provide support.** This might include friends, family members, teachers, or coaches.
- **Communicate your goals to them.** Let them know what you're aiming for and how they can help.
- **Arrange regular check-ins.** Whether it's weekly coffee with a mentor or daily text updates with a friend, consistent communication keeps you accountable.

Having people in your corner adds another layer of security to your goal-setting process. They're there to pick you up when you fall and to cheer the loudest when you succeed (Health & Wellness Services, 2024).

In essence, the key takeaways here are simple but profoundly impactful: Setting achievable goals, breaking them down into manageable tasks, celebrating small wins, learning from setbacks, and surrounding yourself with a solid support system can significantly boost your confidence. This approach helps foster a positive mindset that can carry you through the ups and downs of teenage life and beyond.

So, let's gear up, set those goals, and celebrate every little victory along the way. Your future self will thank you!

Effective Communication Skills for Asserting Oneself

Effective communication skills are essential for any teenage boy aiming to assert himself and gain confidence in all areas of life. Confidence helps tackle obstacles with resilience and determination, and it's a fundamental trait to develop during these formative years. Let's dive into this with a humorous but practical approach.

First off, let's talk about practicing assertiveness. Knowing how to express your thoughts and feelings clearly and respectfully is the bedrock of assertive communication. Imagine you're at lunch, and you always end up with the soggy piece of pizza because you don't speak up. That's no way to live! Start by voicing your preferences in small, low-stakes situations like choosing the next movie for family night or deciding where to go for ice cream with friends.

Here is what you can do in order to achieve the goal:

- Begin with "I" statements to clearly articulate your thoughts without sounding accusatory, such as "I feel" or "I think."
- Be honest yet tactful. It's not just about what you say but how you say it—try maintaining a calm and steady tone.
- Stick to the point and avoid over- explaining. Simplicity often conveys confidence.

Next up, developing active listening skills is crucial. Think about those times when you're communicating with your parents and they swear you weren't listening. It's frustrating for everyone, right? Active listening isn't just hearing words; it's about understanding the emotions and intentions behind them. Besides making others feel valued, it helps you respond more effectively.

Here is what you can do to become an active listener:

- Focus fully on the speaker and avoid distractions like checking your phone.
- Nod occasionally and use phrases like "I see" or "Uh-huh" to show you're engaged.
- Practice paraphrasing back what the other person says to confirm your understanding, like, "So what you're saying is..."

Now, let's take a crack at using positive body language and vocal tone to convey confidence. Picture this: You're explaining why you should get extra time for homework, but you're slouching, avoiding eye contact, and mumbling. Convincing? Not so much. Your body speaks volumes even when your mouth doesn't. So, stand tall, maintain eye contact, and use a firm yet friendly vocal tone.

Here's what you should aim for:

- Stand or sit up straight without crossing your arms or legs; open posture signals receptiveness.
- Make regular eye contact, but don't turn it into a staring contest—aim for engagement, not intimidation.
- Use gestures to emphasize points but keep them natural and not overly dramatic.
- Maintain a calm, even voice. Think of someone who inspires you and try to emulate their speaking style.

Finally, setting boundaries and expressing needs assertively is the key to establishing healthy communication patterns. Ever had a friend who constantly borrows your stuff and never returns it? It's a boundary issue. Learning to set limits clearly and kindly can save you a lot of stress and resentment down the road. Assertive communication isn't about being selfish; it's about respecting both your needs and the needs of others.

Here's how to set boundaries:

- Clearly state your limits and needs without apologizing; for example, "I need my things back by Friday" is better than "Sorry, but could you maybe return my stuff?"
- Use firm but polite language. Being direct doesn't mean being rude.
- Be consistent. If you set a boundary, stick to it, or people won't take you seriously.

- Practice self-care by prioritizing your own needs from time to time; it's perfectly okay to say "No".

To wrap things up, improving these communication skills will undeniably boost your self-assurance and confidence across various social and personal contexts. Asserting yourself doesn't come naturally to everyone, but with practice, it becomes easier. Remember, every step toward better communication is a leap toward greater confidence. Keep practicing, stay engaged, and always be true to yourself.

CHAPTER 2

Health and Wellness Habits

Leading a Healthy and Balanced Lifestyle

Alright, boys, picture this: you're trying to balance school, sports, a social life, and probably a gaming marathon or two. Suddenly, your mom decides now is a great time to lecture you on "living a healthy lifestyle." You roll your eyes and think, "Yeah, right, like I have time for that." But here's the twist – living a healthy, balanced lifestyle as a teen boy isn't as hard (or lame) as it sounds. In fact, it's more like unlocking a cheat code for feeling unstoppable. Ready to level up? Let's dive in.

So, what's the deal with all this "healthy lifestyle" talk anyway? Imagine you've been glued to your screen for hours, fingers twitching from rapid-fire texting or blasting through digital enemies. Now, fast forward to gym class where even jogging a lap feels like running a marathon. Or maybe you're stressed out because of exams, crushed by anxiety like it's the final boss battle. Sounds familiar? The truth is, ignoring physical exercise can make life way harder. Your body and mind need regular workouts – just like your consoles need updates – to keep running smoothly. Without it, you're not just missing out on those sweet endorphin boosts that make you feel awesome, but also setting

yourself up for some serious health issues down the line.

But don't worry, guys! This chapter will guide you through the maze of prioritizing your well-being, no complicated maps required. We'll explore how regular exercise can be your secret weapon to staying fit and stress-free. We'll talk about cool activities that'll get you moving without feeling like a chore, plus pro tips on integrating fitness into your busy schedule seamlessly. And let's not forget the mental game – we'll uncover how sweating it out can boost your mood, sharpen your focus, and basically turn you into a real-life superhero. So, strap in and get ready to discover how leading a balanced lifestyle is not only doable but downright essential. Time to hit start on a new adventure!

The Importance of Regular Exercise

Alright, imagine you're navigating the whirlwind of schoolwork, social life, and maybe even a part-time job. Now, toss in the daily chaos that comes with screens vying for your attention—video games, social media, you name it. Amidst this hustle, it's easy to let physical and mental well-being take a back seat. However, prioritizing regular exercise can be the game-changer you didn't know you needed. Let's kick things off with the basics: regular exercise not only helps maintain a healthy weight but also strengthens muscles and improves cardiovascular health. Think about it—it's like upgrading your body to the next level. If you've ever felt out of breath after climbing a few flights of stairs or struggled to lift something heavy, that's your body's way of hinting it needs a bit more action. Regular physical activity pumps up your heart rate, gets the blood flowing, and builds those muscles, making everyday tasks much easier (University of Rochester Medical Center, 2024).

Beyond the obvious physical perks, there's a hidden gem in exercise: endorphins. Yes, those magical chemicals your body releases during physical activity that make you feel on top of the world. Endorphins are essentially your body's natural mood lifters. They help improve mental health and reduce the risk of depression (Guo et al., 2022).

Imagine finishing a workout or a game of basketball feeling invincible, like you've conquered a mini-mountain. That's the endorphins at work, giving you a mental boost that makes everything seem a tad more manageable.

Now, let's talk about teamwork, discipline, and confidence. Engaging in sports or fitness activities isn't just about staying fit; it also shapes your character. Being part of a team teaches you the importance of working together towards a common goal. You learn to trust your teammates, communicate effectively, and pick each other up when things go south. Discipline comes into play as you stick to practice schedules and push through tough workouts. And confidence? There's no better feeling than seeing your hard work pay off, whether it's through winning a game or simply improving your skills over time. These experiences build resilience and self-assurance that spill over into other areas of life.

Participating in diverse physical activities is key. We're talking about mixing it up—team sports like soccer or basketball, individual exercises like running or swimming, or even activities that don't necessarily fall into traditional "exercise" categories, like dancing or rock climbing. A varied routine keeps things interesting and works different muscle groups, ensuring overall well-being.

Here is what you can do to keep things exciting:

- Try out different sports or activities to see what you enjoy the most.
- Join clubs or groups where you can meet people with similar interests.
- Set personal goals and challenges to keep yourself motivated.
- Incorporate fun elements, such as music or friendly competitions, into your workouts.

So, what's the bottom line here? You should strive to incorporate a mix of cardiovascular, strength training, and flexibility exercises into your routine for optimal health benefits. Cardiovascular exercises get your heart pumping, strength training builds your muscles, and flexibility exercises improve your range of motion and prevent injuries. It's a trifecta that ensures you're in peak condition both physically and mentally.

To paint a clearer picture, let's break it down a bit more. Cardiovascular exercises could include activities like running, cycling, or even brisk walking. These activities elevate your heart rate and improve lung capacity. Strength training doesn't always mean lifting heavy weights. Bodyweight exercises like push-ups, squats, and planks are highly effective. As for flexibility, think stretching routines, yoga, or Pilates.

These exercises might seem like they belong in the domain of professional athletes or fitness gurus, but they're incredibly accessible to anyone willing to give them a try.

And here's some real talk: starting a new routine can be daunting. It's easy to feel overwhelmed by the idea of dedicating time to exercise, especially when there are so many other distractions. But think of it as an investment in your future self. The habits you form now will stick with you into adulthood, making it easier to stay healthy as you age. Plus, the sense of accomplishment you get from sticking to a routine and seeing progress is truly rewarding. Remember, you don't have to turn into a fitness fanatic overnight. Start small. Maybe it's a 10-minute jog around the block or a quick set of push-ups before bed. Gradually increase the intensity and duration as you get more comfortable. The key is consistency, not perfection.

Also, keep in mind that balance is crucial. Don't push yourself too hard to the point where exercise becomes a chore or causes injury. Listen to your body and give it the rest it needs. Mixing high-intensity workouts with lower-impact activities can help you avoid burnout and keep things enjoyable.

Lastly, let's address the elephant in the room—screen time. It's tempting to spend hours glued to your phone or gaming console, but too much sedentary activity can negate the benefits of exercise. Aim to limit screen time and replace some of it with physical activities.

Trust me, the latest episode of your favorite show will still be there after a good workout.

In conclusion, prioritizing physical and mental well- being through regular exercise sets the foundation for a healthy and balanced lifestyle. It equips you with the tools to handle stress, fosters a sense of accomplishment, and keeps you physically fit. Remember, you're setting the stage for a brighter, healthier

future. So lace up those sneakers, find an activity you love, and start moving. Your body and mind will thank you.

Healthy Eating Habits

When it comes to leading a healthy and balanced lifestyle as a teenage boy, one of the most important aspects is prioritizing your physical and mental well-being. And guess what? A big part of that is eating right! Yes, I know food can be confusing with all the different advice and trends out there, but let's break it down together in a simple, easy-to-understand way.

First off, let's talk about balanced meals. Think of your plate as an artist's palette. You want it bursting with colors from a variety of fruits and vegetables. By doing so, you're ensuring your body gets a wide range of vitamins and minerals which are essential for growth and development. Whole grains like brown rice, oats, and whole wheat bread should also make regular appearances on your plate. These provide the energy you need to power through the day, especially if you're active in sports or other activities. Lean proteins, such as chicken, fish, beans, and nuts support muscle growth and repair, while healthy fats from sources like avocados, olive oil, and nuts keep your brain sharp and your cells healthy (Healthy Eating During Adolescence, 2024).

Now, let's address the sweet stuff and those tempting processed foods.

Limiting sugary drinks, junk food, and foods high in unhealthy fats isn't just about keeping your weight in check; it's about safeguarding your future self from chronic diseases like diabetes and heart disease.

Here's what you can do to cut down on these not-so-nutritious options:

- Swap soda and sugary drinks for water or milk. Even adding a splash of fruit juice to sparkling water can give you a refreshing drink without the excess sugar.

- Reach for snacks like fresh fruits, nuts, or yogurt instead of candy bars or chips.

- Choose grilled or baked options over fried foods whenever possible.

- Read nutrition labels and aim for items lower in added sugars and unhealthy fats.

Another key piece of the puzzle is portion control and mindful eating. This means paying attention to what you eat and how much you eat. It's not about depriving yourself but rather enjoying your food and stopping when you're satisfied, not stuffed. Mindful eating habits might sound a bit "zen," but they really help build a healthier relationship with food.

Here are some tips to get you started:

> - Eat slowly and savor each bite. Put down your fork between bites to pace yourself.
>
> - Pay attention to hunger and fullness cues. It's okay to stop eating when you feel full— even if there's still food on your plate.
>
> - Avoid distractions like smartphones or TV during meals, which can lead to overeating.
>
> - Practice portion control by serving smaller amounts initially. You can always go back for more if you're still hungry.

Ever thought about meal prepping? This isn't just something fitness buffs rave about on social media— it's actually a super practical habit that ensures you have access to nutritious meals even on your busiest days. Meal prepping can prevent you from reaching for fast food or other unhealthy options when hunger strikes.

Here's how you can start:

- Plan your meals for the week ahead, including breakfast, lunch, dinner, and snacks.
- Create a shopping list based on your meal plan to avoid impulse buys.

- Cook larger batches of meals that can easily be stored and reheated throughout the week.
- Pack your meals in portion-sized containers for grab-and-go convenience.

By making informed food choices and prioritizing nutrient-dense foods, you'll be setting yourself up for long-term health benefits. But let's talk about why this matters beyond just your body—your mind matters too. Good nutrition fuels your brain, helps you stay focused in school, reduces stress, and even boosts your mood.

Ultimately, balanced meals filled with colorful fruits and vegetables, whole grains, lean proteins, and healthy fats play a huge role in your growth and development. Reducing sugary drinks and processed foods supports a healthy weight and decreases the risk of chronic diseases. Practicing portion control and mindful eating fosters a positive relationship with food, while meal prepping ensures you always have nutritious options at your fingertips. Remember, it's all about making small, steady changes that add up to significant improvements in your overall well-being. Stick with these practices and you'll be on track to not only being healthy but thriving in all areas of your life.

Managing Stress Through Relaxation

Stress is something we all deal with, but let's be real: being a teenage boy is hard! It's packed with school demands, changing bodies, social pressures, and the occasional home drama. But here's the good news— there are ways to hit pause and manage stress, so it doesn't overwhelm you. And trust me, learning these techniques now will pay off big time later.

Incorporating relaxation practices like deep breathing, meditation, or yoga can seriously help chill you out. I know, I know, meditation might sound a bit too lame for some of you, but hear me out. Just spending a few minutes focusing on your breath can lower your stress levels significantly. Picture this: You're sitting at your desk, overwhelmed by homework. Instead of panicking, take a few deep breaths—in through the nose, out through the mouth. Your heart rate slows down, your mind clears up, and suddenly that mountain of assignments doesn't look so intimidating anymore. It's not magic, it's science (AACAP, n.d.).

Here's what you can do to incorporate these practices:

- Find a quiet spot where you won't be disturbed.
- Sit comfortably or lay down, whichever you prefer.
- Close your eyes and start with deep breathing—draw in breath slowly and fully, and exhale just as slowly.
- Once comfortable with deep breathing, explore apps or online videos that guide you through simple meditations or yoga sessions.
- Make this a daily habit; even 5-10 minutes can make a huge difference.

But if becoming a mini-yogi isn't quite your style, no worries. There are plenty of other ways to relax and de-stress. Engaging in hobbies, creative outlets, or spending time outdoors can work wonders. Whether it's playing an instrument, drawing, biking, or just kicking a soccer ball around, these activities give your mind a vital break from the hustle and bustle. Think about it—when was the last time you were stressed while doing something you genuinely enjoyed?

Exactly. Hobbies act as an escape hatch from the pressures of everyday life.

Now let's talk boundaries and self-care. Managing stress effectively means knowing when to say "No" to extra commitments and giving yourself permission to take care of yourself. It's easy to get caught up in trying to do everything—school, sports, extracurriculars, socializing—but your time and energy are limited resources. Prioritize what matters the most and set limits on things that drain you. If you're feeling swamped, it's okay to skip a hangout session or drop an extra-curricular activity. Your friends might bug you for it, but true friends will get it.

Here's a guideline for setting boundaries and prioritizing self-care:

- Evaluate your current commitments and prioritize them in order of importance and enjoyment.

- Communicate your limits to friends, family, and teachers to avoid over-committing.

- Schedule regular breaks in your day, whether it's for a short walk, reading, or just chilling.

- Don't hesitate to seek support from trusted adults or peers when you're feeling overwhelmed.

And speaking of breaks, let's tackle one of the most underrated yet crucial aspects of de-stressing: sleep. Establishing a bedtime routine and ensuring you get enough sleep is the key to maintaining emotional balance and reducing stress. We live in a world where binge-watching shows till the crack of dawn might seem like a badge of honor, but chronic sleep deprivation is a fast track to Stressville. Start winding down an hour before bed by turning off screens and engaging in calming activities like reading or listening to music. Aim for eight to ten hours of sleep each night. Remember, quality sleep isn't just about quantity— it's also about creating a restful environment.

To break it down, here's how you can improve your sleep routine:

- **Begin winding down an hour before bed by avoiding screens, as the blue light can confuse your brain into thinking it's still daylight.**
- **Engage in calming activities like reading a book, listening to soothing music, or practicing mindfulness exercises.**
- **Make sure your room is dark, cool, and quiet to create an ideal sleeping environment.**
- **Stick to a consistent sleep schedule, even on weekends, to regulate your internal clock.**

These strategies don't just magically happen overnight—they require practice and commitment. But the payoff is worth it. By developing a personalized stress-management plan, you'll have a toolset ready to tackle life's challenges. Remember, it's all about finding what works best for you and sticking with it. No two people handle stress the same way, and that's perfectly normal. Experiment with different techniques, mix and match strategies, and customize your plan. The important thing is to stay proactive and not let stress control your life.

Taking steps to manage stress through relaxation practices, engaging in hobbies, setting boundaries, and establishing good sleep routines are all essential strategies. Incorporating these elements into your daily life will not only help reduce stress but also enhance your overall quality of life. So go ahead, give these tactics a try, and see how much better you feel. After all, a balanced and healthy lifestyle isn't just about surviving your teenage years—it's about thriving in them.

In essence, teenage life is like a roller coaster with its ups, downs, and loop-de-loops. But equipping yourself with effective stress management tools will ensure you enjoy the ride rather than get thrown off course. Stay curious, keep experimenting, and remember—you've got this!

Developing a Positive Body Image

Prioritizing physical and mental well-being is key to leading a healthy and balanced lifestyle as a teen boy. So, let's dive into how you can build a positive body image and a solid self-care routine.

First up, promoting self-acceptance and body positivity is hugely important. Unfortunately, society often pushes a narrow definition of what it means to look "good," but the real truth is everyone is unique and that's fantastic! When you embrace your differences, you start to see them as strengths rather than flaws. Here are some things you can do to foster a healthy self-image and boost your confidence:

- Start by appreciating what your body can do—run, jump, laugh—rather than just focusing on how it looks.
- Find individual features that make you unique and celebrate them.
- Surround yourself with people who uplift you and promote positive vibes.
- Expand your idea of beauty by learning about various cultures and their standards.

Just like tuning up a car keeps it running smoothly, regular hygiene practices, grooming habits, and skincare routines keep you feeling and looking fresh. These practices not only promote physical health but also enhance self-esteem because when you look good, you feel good!

To get started:

- Make it a habit to shower daily. It's amazing how rejuvenating this simple act can be.
- Pay attention to grooming. Whether that's a regular haircut, trimming your nails, or shaving, these little acts go a long way.
- Create a basic skincare routine: cleanse, moisturize, and protect your skin from the sun with SPF.
- Invest in personal care products that suit your needs; trust me, everyone has different skin and hair types.

Now, let's move on to understanding the dangers of body shaming, unrealistic comparisons, and seeking external validation. Living in a world ruled by social media can sometimes mess with your head.

Seeing those heavily filtered selfies and perfectly curated profiles can create impossible standards. Remember, most of those images are staged and edited. Real life is much more diverse and beautiful in its raw form.

Here's the thing—a negative body image can lead to a ton of issues, including depression and poor self-esteem (University, n.d.). Adolescence is already a tricky time physically and mentally, since your body and mind are undergoing significant changes.

Avoiding body shaming and resisting the urge to compare yourself to others can really save you from this trap. Instead, strive to find happiness within yourself rather than waiting for "likes" or validation from others.

The importance of self-love, self-respect, and setting boundaries cannot be overstated. Loving and respecting yourself set the foundation for everything else. It helps you establish your worth and lets you set the right kind of boundaries to protect your mental and emotional health. Here's how to get there:

- Practice self-compassion. Give yourself a break when you mess up. Everyone makes mistakes, and that's okay.
- Respect yourself enough to say "No" to things that bring you down or harm you.
- Set social boundaries. For example, limit how much time you spend on social media, especially if you find yourself constantly comparing yourself to others.
- Start talking to yourself as you would to a best friend. Be kind, encouraging, and supportive.

So, what's the takeaway? As a teenage boy, prioritizing self-care practices and cultivating a healthy body image while practicing self-compassion will massively contribute to your overall wellness and confidence. And hey, it's not just about looking after your body but also nurturing your mind and soul.

Physical activity plays an instrumental role here, too. Engaging in sports or any form of exercise not only keeps you fit but also significantly boosts your self- esteem (Gualdi-Russo et al., 2022). Physical activities provide a sense of accomplishment, making you feel better about your capabilities and, subsequently, your appearance. However, always remember to engage in activities that you enjoy and not just because they are trendy or supposed to "mold" your body into a certain shape.

It boils down to balance. Eating nutritious foods and staying active support your overall health without fixating solely on appearance. Treat exercise as a fun activity rather than a chore. Go play soccer, take a bike ride, or try out dance classes—just keep moving. According to research, maintaining physical activity reduces body dissatisfaction and enhances body satisfaction (Artigues-Barberà et al., 2023).

Moreover, nurture relationships with your family and friends, as they are crucial supporters during your teenage years. Positive connections at home and school are protective factors against unhealthy dieting and negative body image (University, n.d.). Instead of hiding away when things get tough, lean on your loved ones. They're your biggest cheerleaders and can offer valuable advice and encouragement.

Consider journaling as a way to reinforce positive thoughts. Write down things you like about yourself and your achievements, no matter how small they seem.

This practice builds a positive feedback loop, improving your self-confidence over time.

One more thing: always approach media with a critical eye. Recognize that much of what you see is tailored to project an unrealistic image. By being aware of this, you can reduce the impact of harmful comparisons on your self-esteem. Unfollow accounts that make you feel less than stellar, and instead, follow those that inspire and uplift you.

By weaving together all these strands—self- acceptance, good hygiene, mindful media consumption, self-love, and building a strong support network—you'll set yourself up for a balanced and fulfilling life. Each aspect reinforces the other, creating a holistic approach to well-being. In doing so, you not only build a healthier body but also fortify your mind against negativity, giving you a robust sense of self that can withstand societal pressures and challenges.

So go ahead and embrace your quirks, take pride in your efforts, and cultivate a routine that celebrates the complete, unique individual you are!

CHAPTER 3

Practical Skills for Daily Life

Essential Practical Skills

Learning essential practical skills is like having your very own Swiss Army knife – ready for whatever life throws at you. Imagine this: you're on a road trip with friends, the wind in your hair, music blaring, and then BAM – your car grinds to a halt. Suddenly, you're stranded in the middle of nowhere. But instead of panicking, you pop the hood and get to work because you've got the know-how. This chapter is all about equipping you with those invaluable skills that not only save the day but earn you some serious respect from your peers.

Picture another scenario: it's game night, and your team is counting on you to host the FIFA showdown. Just as everything's about to kick off, there's an ominous sound from the plumbing, followed by water spraying everywhere. That's a level of chaos no teenage boy wants to face unprepared. Or, consider navigating the tricky waters of financial independence – knowing how to budget your allowance could mean the difference between scoring that new game release or being left penniless by the snack machines. Without these essential skills, minor inconveniences can quickly spiral into full-blown crises.

In this chapter, we'll dig into basic auto mechanics so you can handle oil changes, tire troubles, and unexpected breakdowns like a pro. You'll also get a crash course in home repairs – mastering tools, fixing leaks, and tackling minor electrical issues, making you the household hero. Finally, we'll talk money: budgeting, saving, and understanding credit to set you up for a financially stable future. By the end of this chapter, you'll be armed with the confidence and knowledge to tackle daily challenges head-on. Roll up your sleeves; it's time to dive in and become the ultimate problem-solver!

Basic Auto Mechanics and Maintenance

First up, let's talk about teaching teens how to check and change oil in a car. Now, I know what you're thinking – "Oil changes? Seriously?" But trust me, it's not as intimidating as it sounds. Imagine the sense of independence you'll have, not having to wait around for an expensive mechanic when you could be out there doing stuff that actually interests you. Here's what you can do in order to achieve the goal:

- **First, make sure your car is parked on level ground and the engine is cool.** You don't want to burn yourself. Safety first!
- **Locate the oil dipstick** – usually marked with a bright color like yellow or orange. Pull it out, wipe it clean, and then reinsert it fully before pulling it out again to check the oil level. If it's below the minimum mark, it's time for an oil change.
- **Place an oil pan under the oil drain plug** – located under the car. This catches the old oil. Use a wrench to remove the plug and let all the oil drain out. Be patient; this takes a few minutes.
- **Once drained, replace the drain plug tightly and move on to the oil filter. Remove the old filter** (it might be hand-

tightened), and smear a little bit of new oil on the rubber seal of the new filter before installing it.

- **Pour in the new oil using a funnel,** checking the dipstick periodically to ensure you're adding the right amount. Easy peasy!
- **Finally, clean up any spills, double-check everything is tightened, and recycle the old oil responsibly.**

Next, let's dive into the ever-so-thrilling world of tire pressure and changing flat tires. Trust me, nothing says "I've got this" quite like knowing you can handle a blowout on your own. Plus, proper tire maintenance ensures better gas mileage and improved handling. Consider it the automotive version of having good shoes.

Here's what you can do:

- **Keep a tire pressure gauge handy.** Regularly check your tire pressure, especially before long trips. The correct pressure information is often found inside the driver's door frame.
- **To change a flat, first, find a safe place to pull over.** Engage the parking brake and use wheel wedges if available. These steps are crucial for preventing the car from rolling.
- **Locate your spare tire, jack, and lug wrench** – usually found in the trunk. Consult the owner's manual if needed.
- **Use the lug wrench to loosen the lug nuts** slightly while the car is still on the ground. Don't remove them just yet.
- **Position the jack under the car's frame** nearest to the flat tire and lift the vehicle until the flat tire is off the ground.

- **Now, fully remove the lug nuts and get the flat tire off.** Mount the spare tire onto the lug bolts and tighten the lug nuts by hand first.
- **Lower the car back to the ground and finish tightening the lug nuts in a star pattern to ensure even pressure.**

These skills will empower you to handle common automotive issues confidently and efficiently.

Now, let's discuss the importance of regular vehicle inspections and basic troubleshooting techniques. It's all about preemptive action – catching minor problems before they become major headaches (and wallet-drainers).

Start by getting familiar with your car. Listen to it, feel it, and pay attention to anything that seems off. For instance, unusual noises, odd smells, or fluid leaks are red flags. If something feels different – like a change in braking, acceleration, or steering – don't ignore it.

Here's how to keep things in check:

- **Regularly inspect your vehicle's lights, signals, and windshield wipers.** These small components are vital for safety and visibility.
- **Check fluid levels** – including coolant, brake fluid, transmission fluid, and windshield washer fluid. Topping them off when necessary keeps your car running smoothly.
- **Inspect belts and hoses for signs of wear and tear.** Cracks or fraying can lead to bigger issues if left unaddressed.
- **Make sure your battery terminals are clean and secured.** Corrosion can cause starting problems and affect your car's electrical system.

- Every couple of weeks, take a minute to walk around your vehicle and visually inspect the tires for any embedded objects and abnormal wear patterns.

Lastly, let's talk about assembling an emergency kit for your car. Think of it as your automotive first aid kit – essential for those "just in case" moments. Having this kit can save the day when you least expect it.

Here's what your kit should include:

- **A spare tire, jack, and lug wrench** – because flat tires happen more often than you'd think.
- **Jumper cables** – dead batteries are the worst, especially when you're far from home.
- **A tire pressure gauge** – keeping tire pressure in check can prevent flats.
- **A multi-tool** – because you never know when you might need a screwdriver, pliers, or a knife.
- **Road flares or reflective triangles** – crucial for signaling caution to other drivers if you're stuck on the side of the road after dark.
- **Basic first aid supplies** – bandages, antiseptic wipes, and pain relievers can come in handy for minor injuries.
- **Flashlight and extra batteries** – seeing clearly can make all the difference in an emergency.
- **Non-perishable snacks and water** – if you're stranded, staying hydrated and having a snack can help keep you calm and focused.

- **Gloves and a blanket** – in case you have to brave the cold for a prolonged period.

Automotive First Aid Kit

- Spare tire
- Jack
- Lug Wrench
- Tire Pressure Gauge
- Multi-Tool
- Reflective Triangles
- Basic First Aid
- Jumper Cables
- Flash lights & Extra Battery
- Snacks & Water
- Gloves & Blanket

By mastering these basics of auto mechanics, you can save yourself – and possibly your friends – from expensive repairs and stressful situations. You'll gain valuable life skills that enhance self-reliance and problem-solving capabilities. An empowered driver is a confident driver, ready to tackle whatever the road throws your way. So, roll up those sleeves and dive in – not only will you learn a lot, but you'll also realize that taking care of a car isn't just a task; it's a step toward being independent and prepared for life's big journey.

Essential Home Repair and DIY Skills

Let's jump right into why learning some home repair and DIY skills is not just cool, but essential. Imagine this: you're at home, alone, and suddenly, there's water spraying everywhere from a busted faucet. Panic mode, right? Not if you've got the basic skills to handle it!

Understanding Basic Tools for Household Repairs

Getting Familiar with Essential Tools

If you've ever found yourself puzzled over which tool to use for a simple household repair, you're not alone. The first step is to acquaint yourself with the basic tools commonly used in these situations. Take it slow and start by getting to know essential tools, such as a hammer, screwdrivers (both flathead and Phillips), pliers, and a wrench. These tools are versatile and likely to be your go-to instruments for various tasks around the house.

The Multi-Purpose Hammer

Let's begin by exploring the classic tool - the hammer. A hammer is a versatile tool with a heavy head attached to a long handle. It is primarily used for driving nails into various surfaces or extracting them if needed. Before using a hammer, ensure you have a firm grip on the handle and position the head accurately to avoid any mishaps.

Unraveling the Mystery of Screwdrivers

Next up, let's delve into the world of screwdrivers. There are primarily two types you should be familiar with - the flathead and

Phillips screwdrivers. The flathead screwdriver features a single, flat blade ideal

for screws with a straight-line cut, while the Phillips screwdriver has a cross-head design suitable for corresponding screws. Understanding the right screwdriver for the job will save you time and frustration during repairs.

The Handy Pliers

Moving on to pliers, these versatile tools come in various shapes and sizes, each designed for specific tasks. Pliers are handy for gripping, bending, or cutting objects, such as wires, pipes, or small items that are challenging to handle with bare hands. It's essential to use the right type of pliers for the job, ensuring a secure grip and efficient handling of materials.

Mastering the Wrench

Last but not least, let's shine a light on the wrench. A wrench is a tool used to provide grip and mechanical advantage in applying torque to turn objects like nuts and bolts. There are various types of wrenches, each serving a unique purpose. Understanding how to select the correct wrench size and type for different tasks will enhance your efficiency and productivity in household repairs.

While these tools may seem basic, mastering their use is essential for tackling everyday repair tasks effectively. Practice using each tool in different

scenarios to build confidence and familiarity. As you become more comfortable handling these basic tools, you'll find yourself better equipped to take on a wide range of household repair projects with ease.

Creating a home repair toolkit is another great step. Building your own toolkit feels like assembling a mini arsenal; you'll be ready for anything. Start with the basics:

- A hammer
- Screwdrivers (flathead and Phillips)
- Pliers
- Adjustable wrench
- Measuring tape

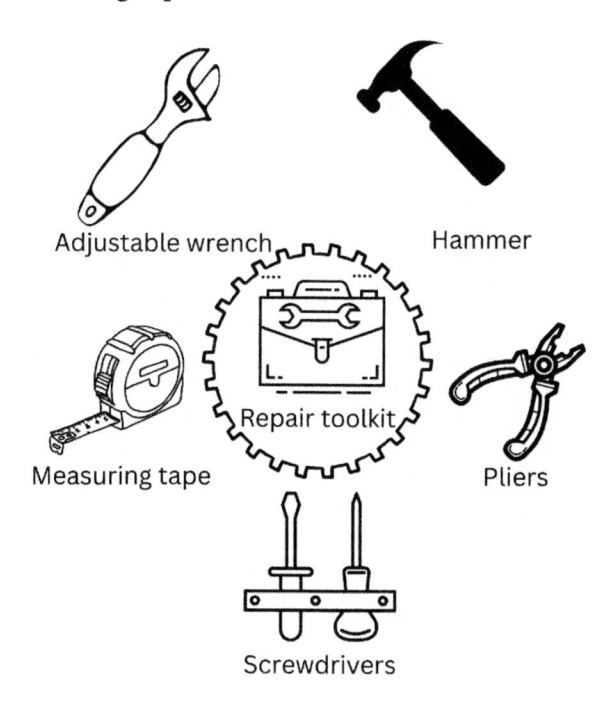

Adjustable wrench
Hammer
Measuring tape
Repair toolkit
Pliers
Screwdrivers

These should cover most minor repairs. Add tools as you learn more skills. Resources for advanced DIY skills are abundant online. Websites, YouTube tutorials, and even local community classes can offer detailed guides on pretty much anything. You can also volunteer with groups like Habitat for Humanity to gain hands-on experience (Learn Basic Home Maintenance and Repairs, n.d.).

By taking the time to understand and familiarize yourself with essential tools like hammers, screwdrivers, pliers, and wrenches, you'll be well- prepared to tackle common household repairs confidently. The key lies in practice and hands-on experience, so don't hesitate to roll up your sleeves and dive into your next repair project armed with newfound knowledge and skills.

Next, safety measures and precautions. This part might seem like the least fun, but unless you fancy a trip to the ER, pay attention. When working on any DIY project:

- **Wear safety goggles** when cutting or drilling. Your eyes will thank you.
- **Gloves protect your hands** from splinters, cuts, or chemical burns. Plus, they make you look cooler, like a pro.
- **Know where the main water and electricity shut-offs are.** You don't want to be fumbling around during an emergency.
- **Use ladders properly** —don't stand on the top rung, keep them stable, and have someone spot you if possible.

Here's what you can do to get started:

Fixing Minor Electrical Issues

Most minor electrical issues can be easily solved if you know what you are dealing with. These could be tasks as simple as changing a light switch or fixing a broken lamp. The key is to identify the problem correctly before attempting any repairs. Before attempting any work on electrical components, it is crucial to prioritize safety. Always remember to shut off the power supply to the area you are working on. This prevents any risk of electric shock and ensures your safety throughout the repair process.

Changing a Light Switch

When it comes to changing a light switch, the process is relatively straightforward. Start by turning off the power from the main source. After confirming the power is off using a voltage tester, remove the cover plate and unscrew the switch from the electrical box. Take note of the wire placements on the existing switch before disconnecting them and connecting them to the new switch in the same way. Finally, secure the new switch in place, attach the cover plate, and restore power to test the new switch.

Fixing a Broken Lamp

Fixing a broken lamp can also be a common electrical issue at home. Begin by unplugging the lamp to ensure there is no power running to it. Carefully inspect the lamp for any visible damage, such as a frayed cord or a loose connection. If the issue lies with the cord, it can be replaced easily by purchasing a new cord of the same type and wattage. For loose connections, tighten any screws or connectors to ensure a secure fit. Once the necessary repairs are made, plug the lamp back in and test it to ensure it is working properly.

Remember, while these tasks may seem simple, it is always important to approach them with caution and follow safety procedures to avoid any accidents or damage.

By understanding the problem, prioritizing safety, and following step-by-step instructions, you can effectively address minor electrical issues in your home.

Fixing a Loose Cabinet Door

When you notice a cabinet door in your home is loose, it can be frustrating. The first step is to understand what is causing the problem. Often, it is a simple matter of a loose screw. Taking the time to inspect the cabinet door closely can help you identify the specific issue you are facing.

To fix a loose cabinet door, you will need a basic tool: a screwdriver. A screwdriver is a simple handheld tool that allows you to tighten or loosen screws easily. By having the right tool at hand, you can tackle the problem quickly and efficiently.

Once you have identified the loose screw causing the cabinet door to be unstable, it's time to take action. Using your screwdriver, carefully tighten the screw by turning it clockwise. Make sure not to overtighten the screw, as this can cause damage to the cabinet door or the surrounding frame.

After tightening the screw, it's essential to test the cabinet door to ensure it is once again secure. Open and close the door several times to check for any remaining issues. If the door feels stable and no longer wobbles, you have successfully fixed the problem.

To prevent future issues with loose cabinet doors, it's important to perform regular maintenance. Check all the screws and hinges on your cabinet doors periodically to ensure they are secure. Tighten any loose screws promptly to avoid more significant problems down the line.

By taking the time to fix a loose cabinet door, you can enjoy the satisfaction of completing a simple home improvement project. Not only will the cabinet door look better, but you will also have the peace of mind knowing that you have taken care of a small repair on your own.

Fixing a Leaky Faucet

To fix a leaky faucet, start by turning off the water supply. This step is super important because if you don't, you might end up with a kitchen that looks like a waterpark. Imagine all the water gushing out uncontrollably if you forget this crucial step. So, find the water shut-off valves under the sink or in the bathroom, turn them tightly clockwise to close them, and make sure no water flows from the faucet.

Gathering the necessary tools is the next step in fixing that annoying leak. You'll need simple tools like an adjustable wrench, a screwdriver, and maybe some plumber's tape for good measure.

These tools are like your trusty sidekicks in your quest to conquer the leaky faucet monster.

Once you've got the water supply turned off and your tools ready, it's time to investigate the leaky culprit. Check the faucet carefully to identify where the leak is coming from. Is it a drip from the spout, a leak near the base, or water spraying everywhere? Understanding the source of the leak will help you determine the best course of action to fix it.

Now comes the slightly tricky part - disassembling the faucet. Don't worry; it's not as intimidating as it sounds. Use your tools to carefully remove the handle and any other parts of the faucet that are hiding the internal components. Take your time and pay close attention to how everything fits together. You might want to take a picture as a reference in case you forget how to reassemble later.

Once you've identified the problem and disassembled the faucet, it's time to replace any faulty parts. This could be a worn-out washer, a damaged O-ring, or a corroded valve. Consult your local hardware store or a plumbing expert to find the right replacement parts for your specific faucet model. Installing the new parts correctly is crucial to ensuring your faucet stops leaking for good.

With the new parts in place, it's time to put everything back together. Follow the reverse order of how you took the faucet apart, referring to your photos if needed. Make sure each component fits snugly and securely to avoid any future leaks. Tighten the screws, reattach the handle, and give everything a final once-over to ensure nothing is out of place.

The moment of truth has arrived - turn the water supply back on and test your handiwork. Slowly open the faucet to check for any leaks or drips. If everything looks good and the leak has been banished, pat yourself on the back for a job well done. However, if the leak persists, it might be time to call in a professional plumber for some expert help.

Before declaring victory over the leaky faucet, do a final inspection to ensure everything is functioning as it should. Listen for any unusual sounds, check for any loose parts, and make sure there are no water puddles forming under the sink. It's better to be safe than sorry, so take your time to double-check everything before considering the job complete.

Putting It Into Action

Now, let's get those handyman hands dirty with unclogging drains, changing air filters, and routine maintenance tasks. Who hasn't experienced the horror of a clogged drain? It's nasty but manageable. Get yourself a drain snake or even a good old plunger. Stick the snake down there, twist and pull out the gunk. Done.

For air filters, they're usually found in your heating or AC units. Just slide the old one out and pop a new one in. Bam, your house breathes better. Routine stuff like checking smoke detectors, sealing drafts, and even replacing batteries falls here too. It might sound dull, but these small actions save big bucks.

Learning these skills empowers you. There's nothing quite like the feeling of fixing something yourself. It's practical, saves money, and boosts your confidence. You stop seeing problems as obstacles and start seeing them as challenges to overcome. Plus, the more you know, the less you'll need to rely on professionals for every little issue.

There's an added bonus: working on home projects can also be a great way to spend quality time with family or friends. Get together to fix a fence, build a birdhouse, or repaint a room. It's productive and strengthens bonds.

And let's address the obvious: being able to handle home repairs makes you a hero in your own home. Parents are impressed, siblings are grateful, and you feel like you've got superpowers when no one else knows how to tackle a problem. Overall, by having these home repair and DIY skills, you're prepping yourself for life. It's about personal growth and grasping real-world knowledge that's applicable daily. From saving money on services to overcoming fears of the unknown, these skills give you self-reliance. Next time a pipe bursts or a light flickers out, you won't break a sweat. You'll grab your tools, don your safety gear, and head into the fray with confidence. And if you mess up? Oh well, good thing you know where the hardware store is!

So, roll up those sleeves and dive into some DIY adventures. Your future self will thank you. And who knows? Maybe you'll even enjoy the process enough to pass these skills down to others, becoming the go- to fixer-upper in your friend group or family.

Remember, the journey of a thousand miles starts with a single step—or in this case, a single tightened screw.

Financial Literacy and Money Management

You've probably been told once or twice that money doesn't grow on trees. Well, unless you have a very peculiar sort of apple tree in your backyard, it's true. Money is something you earn, save, and spend carefully. This means financial literacy is critical for young men like you to tackle real-life challenges head-on. Let's break it down.

Starting with the basics, think of budgeting as your financial GPS—it helps you navigate where your money should go. First off, figure out how much money you're making, whether it's from an allowance, part-time job, or some other source. Got that? Great. Now, let's talk about where it's all going. Are you spending mostly on essentials like food and school supplies, or is your money mysteriously vanishing into the black hole of snack machines and video games?

Here is what you can do in order to achieve better budgeting:

- **Begin by jotting down every expense for a week.** Yes, even those sneaky costs like that soda you bought at lunch.
- **Next, categorize these expenses.** Which ones were absolutely necessary, and which ones could you live without?
- **Set up a simple budget.** Allocate part of your income to essentials, another chunk to savings, and leave a little wiggle room for fun stuff.
- **Stick to your budget!** Track your spending and adjust as needed. Think of this like leveling up in a video game; the more you practice, the better you'll get.

Now, the importance of setting financial goals can't be overstated. Without goals, you're just floating aimlessly through the fiscal sea, hoping not to drown in debt. A solid goal might be saving up for a car, college, or even that latest gadget you've been eyeing. But here's the catch—you need to understand the concept of credit before diving too deep.

Credit can be a helpful tool, but it's a double-edged sword. If used responsibly, it can help you buy things now and pay later, like taking out loans for education or using a credit card for emergencies. However, misuse it, and you could end up in a heap of debt. It's crucial to understand the difference between good debt (like student loans) and bad debt (like unpaid credit card balances). The goal is to build a good credit score, which will make life a lot easier when it comes to bigger purchases like a house or car loan.

Speaking of loans, ever heard of compound interest? It's like magic—except it's math! The earlier you start saving, the more your money will grow over time thanks to this magical beast. Imagine you save a small amount regularly. Due to compound interest, not only do you earn interest on the money you put in, but also on the interest it earns. Start early, and your future self will thank you big time. Just imagine being able to afford those dream vacations or that sleek sports car faster than your peers!

To really drive this point home, consider that every financial decision you make today impacts your future goals. For example, blowing your entire paycheck on fast food and concert tickets may give you immediate gratification, but it doesn't help you save for a new computer or set you up for financial independence. Understanding the benefits of saving early is the ticket to achieving your long-term dreams.

So, how do you get started on this path? Opening a bank account is a fantastic first step. Not only does it provide a safe space for your money, but it also gives you access to tools like online banking and budgeting apps to track your expenses. Most banks offer youth accounts, which usually come with lower fees and educational resources to help you become financially savvy.

Here's what you can do to get started:

- **Visit a local bank or credit union to learn about their youth account options.** Ask questions about fees, interest rates, and online banking features.
- **Open an account with a parent or guardian if you're under 18.** They'll co-sign, meaning they'll keep an eye on your finances too.
- **Start depositing a portion of your income or allowance regularly.** It might seem boring, but trust me, watching your savings grow can be incredibly satisfying.
- **Use online tools to track your expenses.** There are plenty of free apps out there designed to help you see exactly where your money is going.

Managing your allowance and tracking your expenses are vital skills. These habits form the bedrock of good financial practices you'll carry throughout your life. Try setting aside a fixed percentage of your allowance for savings right away and use the rest wisely. If you start managing small amounts of money well, scaling up won't be that difficult as you grow older.

Let's not forget about staying out of debt traps. One common pitfall is impulsive spending—yes, those spontaneous buys during a mall outing. Train yourself to recognize impulse purchases versus necessary expenditures. Creating a list before shopping or setting a waiting period before buying non-essential items can curb those urges.

By gaining solid financial literacy skills, you position yourself to make informed decisions. Think of avoiding debt like dodging pitfalls in a game. Being aware of debt traps helps you sidestep financial woes, leading to greater stability. Just picture yourself graduating from college without an overwhelming pile of debt, or buying your first car without stressing about sky-high interest rates. You'll be thankful for the foundation you built.

In conclusion, learning essential practical skills like financial literacy isn't just about surviving; it's about

thriving. By mastering the basics of budgeting, understanding credit, saving early, and managing your money wisely, you're setting up a stable and prosperous future. It might seem daunting at first, but these skills are as vital as anything else you'll learn in your teenage years. Plus, imagine the satisfaction of knowing your way around money while your friends are still scratching their heads over their next ATM withdrawal. That, my friend, is priceless.

Remember, your financial journey is a marathon, not a sprint. Equip yourself with these skills, apply them diligently, and watch your financial health flourish. Your future self will high-five you for it.

CHAPTER 4

Time Management and Productivity Tips

Effective Time Management

Ever feel like you're constantly running out of time, no matter how hard you try to get everything done? Like you're in a never-ending race against the clock? Well, you're not alone. Managing time effectively can seem like trying to juggle flaming torches while riding a unicycle—it's tough and often feels impossible. But here's the deal: mastering this skill isn't just about squeezing everything into your day; it's about making sure your time is spent on what really matters, leaving room for both responsibilities and fun.

Picture this: you've got a mountain of homework due tomorrow, soccer practice at 5 PM, and that new video game you've been itching to play stares back at you from your desk. The struggle is real. You might find yourself stuck in a vortex of Netflix episodes, knowing you should open those textbooks but just can't muster the willpower. Or maybe you start on your homework but end up down a rabbit hole of cat videos on YouTube. Balancing academics, activities, and personal life isn't just challenging it can feel downright chaotic without a good plan.So, what's the secret to not losing your mind in this whirlwind? This chapter dives into creating daily schedules and prioritizing tasks to help you maximize productivity. You'll learn how to establish routines, use tools like planners or digital calendars, tackle high-priority items first, and even have some guilt- free breaks. Plus, we'll explore techniques like the Pomodoro method to keep you focused and avoid burnout. By the end, you'll have actionable strategies to turn that crazy juggling act into a well-choreographed performance. Get ready to take control of your time like a boss!

Creating a Daily Schedule and Prioritizing Tasks for Maximum Productivity

Creating a daily schedule and prioritizing tasks for maximum productivity is essential for teen boys to balance academics, activities, and personal life. The trick is not just about fitting everything in but making sure you're spending your time in the best way possible.

First up, establishing a routine. Think of it as building a rhythm for your day, much like setting up a playlist that keeps you grooving from morning till night. Begin by designating specific hours for studying and taking breaks. Believe me, it's not as boring as it sounds. Starting with a solid study block followed by a short, guilt-free break can seriously zap away the feeling of being overwhelmed.

Here's what you can do:

- **Set clear study times:** These are non- negotiable blocks where distractions are minimized, and focus is maximized.

- **Take regular breaks:** Short breaks of 5-10 minutes after every study session help refresh your mind. Use these breaks to stretch, grab a snack, or check your favorite memes—just don't fall into a YouTube rabbit hole!

- **Prioritize tasks:** List out your tasks based on urgency and importance. Homework due tomorrow? That's top of the list. Soccer practice next week? Maybe not so urgent, but still important. Tackling high-priority items first ensures you're not pulling an all-nighter later.

Next, let's talk tools. Imagine trying to build something awesome without the right gadgets—time management is no different. Planners and digital calendars are like the ultimate toolset for mapping out your day and allocating specific periods for different activities. Whether you're a paper-and-pen kind of guy or a tech enthusiast, having a visual representation of your day helps keep things organized and manageable.

Here's how to do it:

- **Choose your tool:** It could be a classic planner or an app like Google Calendar or Todoist. What matters is what works best for you.

- **Block off time:** Allocate chunks of time for various activities like classes, homework, sports, and chilling out. Seeing everything laid out can help you avoid overcommitting and ensure there's time for everything.
- **Sync up:** If you go digital, sync your calendar across devices, so whether you're on your phone or at your laptop, you're always in the know about what's coming up next.

Another key technique in your arsenal should be the Pomodoro method. This technique is less about fancy names and more about maximizing productivity while keeping burnout at bay. It involves working in focused intervals—usually around 25 minutes—followed by short breaks.

To get started:

- **Pick a task:** Decide what you need to work on.
- **Set a timer for 25 minutes:** Focus solely on that task until the timer goes off.
- **Take a 5-minute break:** Step away from your work, stretch, relax.
- **Repeat:** After four intervals, take a longer break—about 15-30 minutes.

This method not only boosts efficiency but also makes long study sessions feel less daunting. Plus, there's something oddly satisfying about racing against a timer, right?

Finally, reflecting on your daily schedule is crucial. It might sound a bit clichéd, but taking a little time to think about how you've spent your time each day can provide massive insights and help curb those sneaky time-wasting activities.

You can start by:

- **Logging your activities:** Note down how much time you spend on each task throughout the day.

- **Identifying patterns:** Look for any repetitive activities that eat up more time than they should—scrolling through social media, anyone?

- **Re-adjusting your routine:** Shift things around in your schedule to cut out unnecessary time wasters and optimize your productivity.

By consistently scheduling and prioritizing tasks, you can achieve a balanced life that covers academics, extracurricular activities, and personal downtime. Creating a structured daily plan isn't just about boosting productivity; it's about ensuring you have time for everything that matters to you, including having fun.

Remember, balance is key. While smashing those academic goals is important, it's equally vital to carve

out time for activities that make you happy and help you unwind. Whether it's gaming, playing sports, or simply hanging out with friends, these moments are essential for maintaining your overall well-being.

So, grab that planner or fire up your calendar app, and start organizing your life one day at a time. Trust me, once you get the hang of it, managing your time will feel less like a chore and more like a superpower.

Avoiding Procrastination and Staying Focused on Goals

Avoiding procrastination and staying focused on goals can be a real struggle, especially when balancing academics, activities, and personal life. Let's crack this nut together by breaking down some effective strategies that will help you stay ahead of the game.

First, let's tackle the idea of breaking down larger tasks into smaller, more manageable chunks. Picture this: you've got a massive science project due, and just thinking about it makes your brain melt. Instead of trying to swallow the whole thing at once, break it down. Here's what you can do:

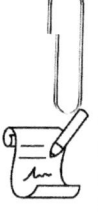

- **Start by outlining all the steps required to complete the project.** This might include researching, writing, creating a visual aid, and preparing to present.

- **Divide these steps into smaller tasks.** For example, research could be broken down into selecting sources, reading materials, and taking notes.

- **Allocate time blocks for each smaller task.** Maybe spend 30 minutes a day researching until it's done.

By dissecting a daunting project into smaller pieces, it stops looking like an undefeatable monster and starts feeling more like a series of doable actions. This approach increases your motivation to start working because each small task completed gives you a sense of achievement, making the larger project less intimidating (Campaign, 2020).

Next, setting deadlines for tasks and holding yourself accountable is crucial. Deadlines give you a clear target, and accountability ensures you keep moving forward. To make this happen, try these steps:

- **Create a timeline for your tasks with specific deadlines for each part.** For example, if your project is due in three weeks, set deadlines for completing research, drafting your report, and finalizing your presentation.

- **Write these deadlines down in a planner or digital calendar.**
- **Share your goals with someone who can help keep you accountable**, like a teacher, friend, or family member.
- **Reward yourself for completing tasks on time**, whether it's treating yourself to a favorite snack or taking a short break (Bokhari et al., 2021).

Addressing the root causes of procrastination is another critical step. Often, we procrastinate out of fear—fear of failure, fear of not doing something perfectly, or simply a lack of interest in the task at hand. While understanding the underlying reasons is essential, developing strategies to combat them can be empowering.

For instance, if it's the fear of failure that's paralyzing you, remind yourself that making mistakes is part of learning and growing. Everyone, even the most successful people, have stumbled before hitting their stride. By facing these fears head-on and using them as learning opportunities, you'll find it easier to stay motivated and focused.

Lastly, practicing self-discipline is vital for effective time management. Self-discipline doesn't mean being hard on yourself; rather, it's about setting boundaries and sticking to them. One technique that works wonders is time blocking.

Here's how you can implement it effectively:

- **Identify the times of the day when you're most productive.** It might be early morning, late afternoon, or after dinner.

- **Allocate specific periods during these times solely for work.** For example, you might block out 4-6 PM every day for homework or study sessions.
- **Minimize distractions during these periods.** Put your phone on silent, close unnecessary tabs on your computer, and let others know you shouldn't be disturbed.

Sticking to these blocks consistently helps create a routine, gradually making it easier to dive into work without the constant battle against procrastination.

It's important to remember that everyone procrastinates from time to time. The key is recognizing when procrastination is creeping in and nipping it in the bud before it grows roots. Combining these strategies—breaking down tasks, setting deadlines, addressing underlying causes, and practicing self-discipline—can transform how effectively you manage your time.

By acknowledging and confronting procrastination, you're already halfway there. For teen boys juggling academics, extracurriculars, and personal interests, mastering time management isn't just about getting

things done—it's about building habits that lead to lifelong success. So next time you feel overwhelmed, remember: take it one step at a time, hold yourself accountable, face your fears, and stay disciplined. You've got this!

Utilizing Technology Tools for Better Time Management and Organization

Navigating the chaos of balancing academics, extracurricular activities, and personal life is no small feat for teenage boys. Imagine you're trying to juggle all those balls without ever letting one hit the ground. Sounds tricky, right? But fear not—technology is here to be your very own juggling assistant! By using productivity apps, digital tools, and time-tracking applications, you can manage your time like a pro. Here's how.

The Power of Productivity Apps

First off, let's talk about productivity apps. These little champions can help streamline how you manage your day-to-day tasks. Visualize this scene: You wake up in the morning, check your phone, and voila! Your entire day's activities are organized into an easy-to- follow to-do list. Not only does this make your day look less daunting, but it also gives you the satisfaction of ticking off tasks as you complete them. Trust me, there's nothing quite like that sweet dopamine rush of crossing items off your list.

Here's what you can do to achieve better organization with productivity apps:

- Start by downloading a well-rated productivity app such as Todoist or Microsoft To Do.
- Create categories for different types of tasks —such as homework, chores, and hobbies.
- Set reminders for each task to ensure you don't end up forgetting something important.

- Track your progress throughout the day to see how effectively you've managed your time.

By doing this, you'll not only feel more in control but will also notice an increase in your overall productivity. After all, who wouldn't want to boost their efficiency while having fun?

Calendar Syncing at Its Finest

Next, let's dive into digital calendar apps. Keeping track of every soccer practice, math assignment deadline, and choir practice can be overwhelming. Synced calendar apps are like having a personal secretary who keeps you on top of everything—minus the suit and tie. When all your devices are synced, you can access your schedule no matter where you are. If you suddenly remember a club meeting while you're out with friends, just pull up your calendar on your phone, and there it is, neatly marked.

Here's how to stay updated on schedules with calendar apps:

- **Choose a reliable calendar app** like Google Calendar or Apple Calendar.
- **Input all your recurring events** such as school hours, club meetings, and sports practices.
- **Make use of color-coding** to differentiate between various types of activities. For example, use blue for academic commitments and green for personal activities.
- **Enable notifications** to receive timely reminders about upcoming events, ensuring you never miss a thing.

Utilizing these features allows you to carry your schedule with you everywhere, making it far easier to navigate through a busy day smoothly. It's like your brain, but with less chance of forgetting!

Time-Tracking for the Win

Ever wonder where all your time goes? One moment you're starting an assignment, and the next, it's bedtime already. Time-tracking apps can help solve this mystery. These apps provide insights into how you spend your time and identify areas where you might be wasting precious minutes—or hours (yes, I'm looking at you, endless scrolling on social media).

Here's how to monitor your time allocation effectively:

- **Download a time-tracking app** like RescueTime or Toggl.
- **Start the timer** whenever you begin a new activity, whether it's studying, playing video games, or hanging out with friends.
- **Review your activity log** at the end of the day to see where most of your time was spent.
- **Look for patterns and identify activities** that consumed more time than necessary. Adjust your schedule accordingly to make room for more productive tasks.

By leveraging time-tracking applications, you'll gain valuable insights into your daily routines and can make necessary adjustments to enhance your time management skills. Think of it as having a mirror that reflects how you truly spend your day.

Task Automation Magic

Finally, let's talk about the magic of task automation. Automating repetitive tasks can save you tons of time and headache, allowing you to concentrate on what truly matters. For instance, setting recurring reminders for weekly assignments or automating file backups gives you more room to breathe and focus on creative endeavors. Imagine having a tool that reminds you every Sunday evening to finish up your science project before Monday. No last-minute panic attacks!

Here's how to integrate technology to simplify your organizational processes:

- **Use tools like Zapier or IFTTT to create automated workflows.** For example, set a workflow that sends you a text reminder every time you receive a new email from your teacher.
- **Incorporate project management platforms** like Trello or Asana to handle group projects and collaborative tasks. Assign roles, set deadlines, and track the project's progress all in one place.
- **Set up automatic file backups** using cloud storage services like Google Drive or Dropbox. This ensures that you always have access to your files, even if your device fails.

Implementing these strategies will transform you into an efficiency wizard, reducing stress and increasing productivity. You'll find that automation isn't just for robots; it's for smart teens too!

Embracing technology for time management and organization isn't just beneficial—it's essential. By incorporating productivity apps, calendar syncingtools, time-tracking applications, and task automation into your daily routine, you can enhance your productivity significantly. Balancing schoolwork, extracurricular activities, and personal time becomes a lot more manageable when you've got these digital allies by your side.

Whether you're aiming for higher grades, mastering a sport, or simply trying to fit in some quality gaming time, effective use of technology can turn the elusive quest for balance into an achievable goal. Let today be the start of your tech-assisted journey toward becoming a time management pro. Now, go ahead and conquer your world!

Balancing Schoolwork, Extracurricular Activities, and Personal Time Efficiently

Effective time management skills are crucial for you to balance academics, activities, and personal life. Let's tackle how you can master this balancing act without losing your mind.

First up, prioritizing tasks based on deadlines and importance. Pretend you've got a big history project due next week, a football game tomorrow, and an urge to binge-watch the latest Netflix series tonight. Seems like a lot, right? Here's a little insider trick: Create a list of all your tasks. Yep, just jot them down. Now, look at which ones are due soonest and which ones hold the most weight, like that history project. It should be up there on your list, alongside your football game. Watching Netflix can wait—it's not going anywhere.

Here's a plan to help you achieve your goal:

- **Start by listing out all your tasks.**

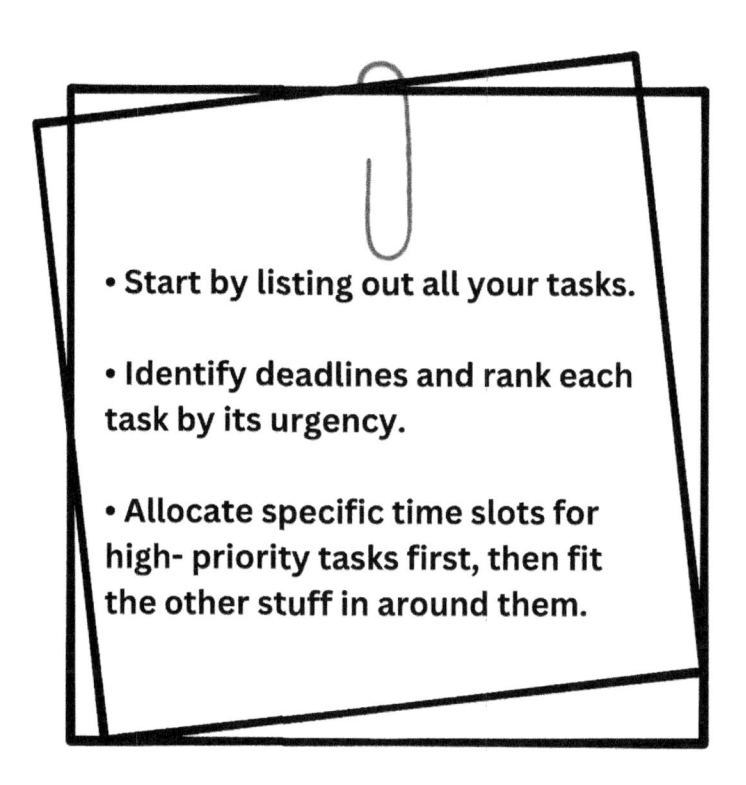

- **Identify deadlines and rank each task by its urgency.**

- **Allocate specific time slots for high- priority tasks first, then fit the other stuff in around them.**

You'd be surprised at how less overwhelming everything becomes once you have it down on paper. Plus, checking things off feels oddly satisfying.

Next, let's talk about implementing a weekly review of your schedule. This one sounds fancy but trust me, it's pretty straightforward and super helpful. Every Sunday evening, sit down with your planner (or phone, if you're into digital tools) and lay out your week. Look at the upcoming deadlines, sports practices, club meetings, and oh, your favorite show's new episode release date too.Here is what you can do in order to achieve the goal:

- Set aside some quiet time on Sunday evenings to plan.

- Review the past week's accomplishments and any pending tasks.
- Adjust your upcoming week's schedule as needed.

This routine keeps you aware of what's coming and prevents nasty surprises that could mess up your perfectly planned Netflix binge.

Now, moving on to developing time management strategies that allow for flexibility. Life happens, right? Maybe you get extra homework dumped on you or your best friend needs help with their own project. Or, more interestingly, your crush finally asks you to hang out. Flexibility is the key here. First, build in buffer times in your schedule—15-minute gaps where you don't plan anything. These gaps will come in handy for unexpected events.

Follow these steps to achieve the goal:

- Add 15-minute buffer periods between major tasks.

- Be willing to swap tasks around when something comes up.

- Reprioritize as necessary while keeping an eye on your most important commitments.

These buffers ensure you're not sacrificing your history project for ice cream with friends unless, of course, you've already nailed that project.

Last but definitely not least, we need to practice effective delegation. If you're swamped with responsibilities, don't hesitate to reach out for help. Maybe your brother can lend a hand with chores, or you can form a study group for that challenging math test. Delegating isn't about being lazy; it's smart resource management.

Here is what you can do in order to achieve the goal:

- Identify tasks that can be shared or delegated.
- Ask for help from peers, family members, or mentors.
- Focus your energy on tasks that require your direct input.

Remember, teamwork makes the dream work. And possibly gives you more time to figure out the perfect way to impress that crush.

Key takeaways? Achieving a harmonious balance between schoolwork, extracurricular engagements, and personal time is absolutely attainable. By structuring schedules, reassessing priorities regularly, and seeking support when necessary, individuals can

optimize their time utilization and maintain a well- rounded lifestyle.

Balancing schoolwork, extracurricular activities, and personal time efficiently isn't just possible—it's totally doable. Think of it like juggling. At first, you might drop a ball or two, but with some practice, you'll be handling those balls like a pro.

Prioritizing tasks teaches you responsibility and helps you focus on what truly matters—those make-or- break deadlines and fitting in time for fun. Speaking of fun, taking a few minutes every week to review and tweak your schedule sets you up for success. Believe it or not, knowing what's ahead can actually reduce stress. You won't have to worry about forgetting that English essay or missing out on basketball practice because your schedule has got your back.

Flexibility is another gem in the treasure chest of time management. Keeping some wiggle room in your plan allows you to adapt to life's ever-changing demands. Your teacher might extend a deadline, or you may get a spontaneous invite from friends; having flexibility means you can adjust without falling behind.

Effective delegation, on the other hand, is about recognizing the power of collaboration. When you're overwhelmed, delegating tasks can lighten your load and foster a team spirit. Learning to ask for help and trust others' abilities doesn't only benefit your time management; it also builds stronger relationships.

The combination of these strategies can seriously level up your time management game. And guess what? When you master these skills now, they'll stick with you for life. Whether it's planning a big project at work, organizing a surprise birthday party for a friend, or ensuring you get quality downtime, these techniques will serve you well.

In the meantime, remember to challenge yourself but also cut yourself some slack. Perfection isn't the goal — a balanced, fulfilling life is. So go ahead, grab that planner, list out your tasks, sprinkle some buffer times, and don't be afraid to call in backup when you need it. With these tricks up your sleeve, you'll be navigating the crazy, wonderful mishmash of teenage life with confidence and ease.

So here's the final thought: every superhero has their own unique way of saving the world, and managing your time effectively lets you be the hero of your own story.

CHAPTER 5

Effective Communication Skills

Enhancing Communication Skills in Teenage Boys

Picture this: You're in the middle of an intense gaming session when your mom calls you downstairs. Annoyed, you half-listen to her lecture about chores while plotting your next move in the game. She finishes talking, and you nod absentmindedly, only to find out later that you agreed to clean the garage for the entire weekend. Sounds familiar? Welcome to the world of communication mishaps! As a teenage boy, navigating conversations can sometimes feel like trying to win a match without a controller. The struggle is real, but don't worry, we've got your back.

Teenage years can often be a whirlwind of misunderstood texts, awkward silences, and "I told you so" moments. Whether it's with friends, family, or even that cute girl from class, expressing yourself clearly isn't always easy. Maybe your buddy feels left out because you didn't invite him to hang out, but instead of saying something, he just gives you the cold shoulder. Or perhaps you've tried explaining to your coach why you missed practice, but your nervous mumbling made it sound like you were speaking a different language. These little miscommunications can quickly snowball into bigger issues, leaving everyone frustrated and feeling unheard.

In this chapter, we're diving headfirst into mastering the art of communication, specifically tailored for teenage boys. We'll explore active listening techniques that will make sure you truly "get" what the other person is saying, boosting both understanding and empathy. Next, we'll tackle assertiveness training, helping you speak your mind without coming off as either a pushover or a bulldozer. And let's not forget non-verbal cues; those tiny gestures and expressions that speak volumes. Finally, we'll arm you with conflict resolution skills to turn heated arguments into productive discussions. By the end of this chapter, you'll be equipped with a toolkit to transform your communication game from "meh" to "legendary." So get ready, because leveling up your conversation skills is about to get a whole lot easier—and maybe even fun!

Improving Understanding and Empathy through Active Listening

Strong communication skills are absolutely critical for building successful relationships and fostering personal growth, especially for teenage boys. Growing up can be a mess of emotions, misunderstandings, and growing pains, but mastering the art of communication can help smooth some of those rough edges. One essential part of this skill set is active listening, which not only deepens your understanding of others but also enhances empathy.

> **Active listening isn't just about hearing words—it's about truly grasping what the other person is trying to convey.**

Imagine you're playing a video game. You can't just watch the screen passively; you need to fully immerse yourself, focus on the objectives, understand the nuances, and remember the details to get to the next level. Active listening works in much the same way. It involves concentrating fully on what's being said, interpreting the information accurately, responding thoughtfully, and remembering the key points.

Here's what you can do to ace active listening:

- **Focus entirely on the speaker.** That means putting your phone away, nodding your head to show you're engaged, and making eye contact.
- **Listen with the intent to understand, not just to reply.** Keep your mind clear of distractions and concentrate solely on the conversation.

Reflecting back what the speaker said serves two purposes: it reinforces your understanding and demonstrates empathy. When someone shares their thoughts or feelings, repeating back their main points shows that you've truly heard them. For instance, if your friend says, "I felt really ignored when no one asked me to join the game," you might respond, "It sounds like you felt left out because no one included you in the game." This kind of response not only clarifies that you've understood but also validates their feelings.

Guideline alert! Here's how to reflect effectively:

- After listening, briefly summarize what they've said in your own words.

- Use phrases like "So what I'm hearing is..." or "It seems like you're saying..."

- Validate their feelings by acknowledging their emotions, saying something like, "That must have been tough."

Asking clarifying questions is another powerhouse tool in active listening. Sometimes, the things people say aren't crystal clear. Maybe your friend mumbles or trails off, or maybe their story is as confusing as a maze. That's where asking questions comes in handy. By seeking clarification, you ensure you've caught every detail and haven't misunderstood anything.

For example, if someone says, "I don't think I can handle it anymore," you might ask, "What do you mean by 'handle it'? Are you talking about school, sports, or something else?" This not only clears up any confusion but also shows that you care enough to dig deeper. Paraphrasing the speaker's words is like hitting the refresh button in a conversation. It not only confirms you've got the message right but also strengthens the connection between you and the speaker. When you paraphrase, you're essentially restating the essence of what's been said in your own words, making sure you're both on the same wavelength.

Here's how to do it:

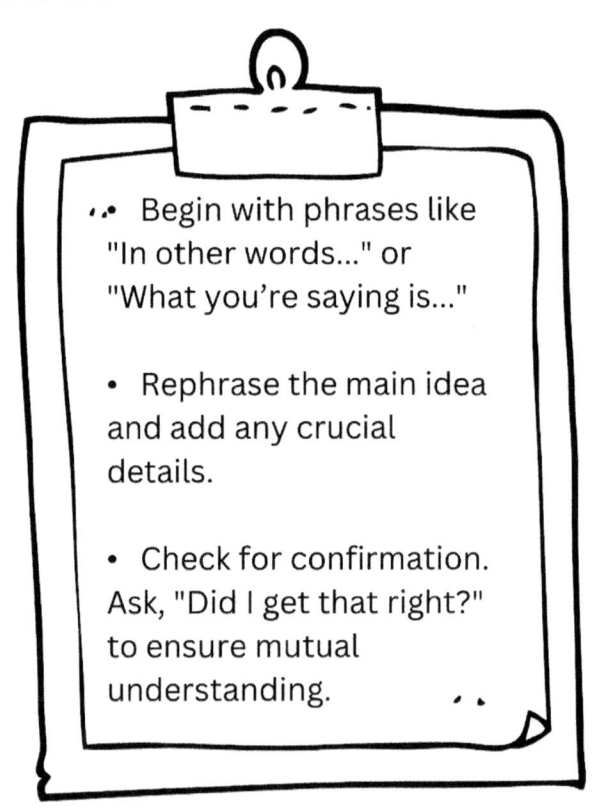

- Begin with phrases like "In other words..." or "What you're saying is..."

- Rephrase the main idea and add any crucial details.

- Check for confirmation. Ask, "Did I get that right?" to ensure mutual understanding.

This brings us to the key takeaways of active listening: it not only boosts your comprehension of the conversation but also significantly enhances empathy—which is like the magic ingredient for better communication. When you actively listen, you're more likely to forge strong, meaningful connections with others, whether it's with friends, family, or even in future romantic relationships.

Imagine you're at lunch with a group of friends. One of them starts talking about a problem they're having with homework. You're tempted to interrupt with a story of your own. But instead, you decide to practice active listening. You focus on them, nod along, and maybe throw in a "Yeah, that sounds frustrating" to keep them going. When they pause, you might ask, "What's been the hardest part for you?"—giving them another chance to share more deeply. By the end of lunch, not only have you learned more about your friend, but you've also shown them that you genuinely care. Plus, they'll probably be more inclined to listen to your stories too!

Active listening is an all-encompassing communication skill that builds trust, promotes empathy, and fosters genuine human connection. Remember, it's about focusing intently, responding thoughtfully, and maintaining presence in the conversation. It's like forming a high-score combo in life; each step you take adds to your overall success in relationships and personal growth.

So go ahead, give these techniques a shot. Practice with friends, family, or anyone willing to chat. You'll find the payoff—building trust, understanding, and empathy—is well worth the effort. You might feel a bit awkward at first, but like learning anything new, it gets easier with time and consistent practice. And before long, you'll be navigating social interactions like a seasoned pro, all while making your relationships stronger and more fulfilling.

Developing Clear and Respectful Communication through Assertiveness Training

Strong communication skills are essential for successful relationships and personal growth in teenage boys. For starters, developing clear and respectful communication through assertiveness training is a game changer. Now, I know what you might be thinking—"Assertiveness? That's just a fancy word for being pushy, right?" Well, not quite. Let's delve into what assertiveness really means and why it's crucial for you.

Wheel Of Emotions

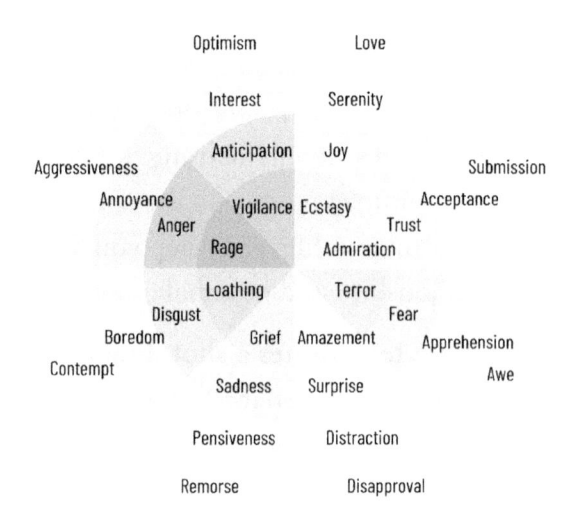

```
                    Optimism        Love
                    Interest        Serenity
                    Anticipation    Joy
   Aggressiveness                                Submission
        Annoyance         Vigilance  Ecstasy    Acceptance
             Anger                     Trust
                    Rage            Admiration
                    Loathing        Terror
             Disgust                     Fear
        Boredom          Grief  Amazement       Apprehension
   Contempt                                          Awe
                    Sadness         Surprise
                    Pensiveness     Distraction
                    Remorse         Disapproval
```

Idea 1: Assertiveness involves expressing thoughts, feelings, and needs honestly and respectfully.

Alright, let's kick things off by understanding that assertiveness isn't about bulldozing over people to get your way. Think of assertiveness as a superpower—a way to express your own thoughts, feelings, and needs without turning into the Hulk or shrinking away like Ant-Man. It's all about balance. Here's what you can do in order to achieve this:

- **Start by being honest with yourself and others.** If something bothers you, say it—just make sure you're not turning it into an attack.
- **Respect is key.** You're not the only one with thoughts and feelings, so remember to acknowledge the other person's perspective too.
- **Use clear and direct language.** Vague hints work great in mystery novels but not so much in real life.

> **Idea 2:** Using "I" statements can help convey thoughts and emotions without blaming others.

This brings us to a nifty little tool called "I" statements. Instead of saying, "You never listen to me," try flipping it to "I feel ignored when you don't listen." See the difference? The first one sounds like an accusation while the second is more about how you feel. It's less likely to make the other person defensive and more likely to lead to an effective conversation.

Here is what you can do:

- **Begin with "I feel" followed by your emotion.** Example: "I feel frustrated."

- **Add the specific action that caused this feeling.** Example: "I feel frustrated when my ideas are interrupted."
- **Conclude with why this matters to you.** Example: "I feel frustrated when my ideas are interrupted because I want to contribute to the discussion."

Trust me, making this small change in how you talk can dramatically improve how well you're understood and how well others respond to you.

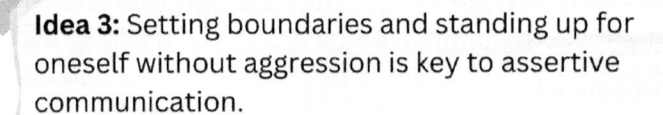

> **Idea 3:** Setting boundaries and standing up for oneself without aggression is key to assertive communication.

Setting boundaries is like putting up a fence around your personal space—not a brick wall, but a nice picket fence with a gate. It's about standing up for yourself without turning into Godzilla. For instance, if a friend habitually borrows your stuff without asking, it's alright to say, "I'd appreciate it if you could ask before taking my things." No need to breathe fire, a simple request will suffice.

To effectively set boundaries:

- **Clearly state what you need or expect.** For example, "I need some downtime after school before starting on homework."
- **Be consistent.** If you sometimes allow the boundary to be crossed, it sends mixed messages.
- **Stay calm and composed.** Getting angry or upset weakens your position and makes it harder to stand firm.

And remember, boundaries are there to protect your well-being and maintain healthy relationships. There's nothing unkind about them.

> **Idea 4:** Practicing assertive responses in various scenarios can help build confidence in communication.

Lastly, let's talk about practice. Yep, just like with sports or learning to play an instrument, practicing assertive communication can make you better at it. Imagine different scenarios you might find challenging—maybe asking someone to return borrowed money, or standing up to a bully. Try role-playing these situations with a friend or even in front of a mirror (no judgment here, everyone does it).

Here are some ways to practice:

- **Role-play different scenarios with someone you trust.** Taking turns playing both roles can give you insight into how the other person might feel and react.
- **Use a mirror to observe your body language and facial expressions.** Confident posture and steady eye contact are just as important as the words you say.
- **Write out assertive responses ahead of a difficult conversation.** This preparation can reduce anxiety and help you stay focused during the actual interaction.

The more you practice, the more natural assertiveness will feel. Before you know it, you'll be navigating tricky conversations with ease and confidence.

Assertiveness empowers teenage boys to communicate effectively while respecting themselves and others. It's a blend of honesty, respect, and balance, not an excuse to be demanding or aggressive. By using "I" statements, setting clear boundaries, and practicing various scenarios, you can develop a strong foundation in assertive communication. Remember, it's not about winning arguments but about creating an environment where mutual respect thrives.

To sum it up, assertiveness is like adding a turbo boost to your communication skills, allowing you to express yourself clearly and confidently. So go ahead, embrace your inner superhero, and start practicing today. You'll find that not only do your relationships improve, but your self-esteem gets a solid boost too. And who doesn't want that?

Increasing Awareness of Non- Verbal Cues and Body Language

Alright, let's have a chat about something many teenage boys might not think too much about but that's actually super important— non-verbal cues and body language. First off, you've probably heard adults say things like, "It's not what you said, it's how you said it." Turns out there's a whole lot of truth in that. Your body often speaks louder than your words.

Understanding body language can provide additional insight into a person's feelings and intentions. Imagine you're talking to your best friend about a guitar you saw in the music store. He's nodding and saying, "Yeah, sounds cool," but his arms are crossed, and he's looking away. His words say he's interested, but his body says, "not really." This mixed signal is where non-verbal cues come into play.

Now, if you want to step up your communication game, eye contact and posture are key. Ever noticed how when someone stands tall and looks you in the eyes, you take them more seriously? That's because eye contact shows confidence and interest. Think about it: would you trust someone who can't meet your gaze during a conversation? Probably not.

Here's what you can do to get this down:

- **Start by maintaining eye contact for a comfortable length of time.** Not like a staring contest, just enough to show you're engaged.
- **Stand or sit up straight.** Good posture makes you appear more confident and attentive.

Easy stuff, right? But it makes a big difference. Gestures, facial expressions, and tone of voice also play a significant role in how your message is received. Say you're telling a joke. If you're grinning ear-to-ear and using an animated voice, it's way funnier than if you're stone-faced and mumbling. So, next time you're trying to make someone laugh or simply tell a story, let your face and hands do some of the talking. It adds color and emotion to your words.

But here's a tip: Be mindful of overdoing it. Too many wild gestures can distract from your message. It's a balance, like seasoning your favorite dish. You want just the right amount for it to taste great.

Paying attention to non-verbal signals helps in adjusting communication styles for better outcomes. Let's say you're asking your teacher for extra credit. If she's leaning forward, nodding, and smiling, she's open to your request. But if she's sitting back, arms folded, and sighing, you might need to rethink your approach.

Here's how to adjust:

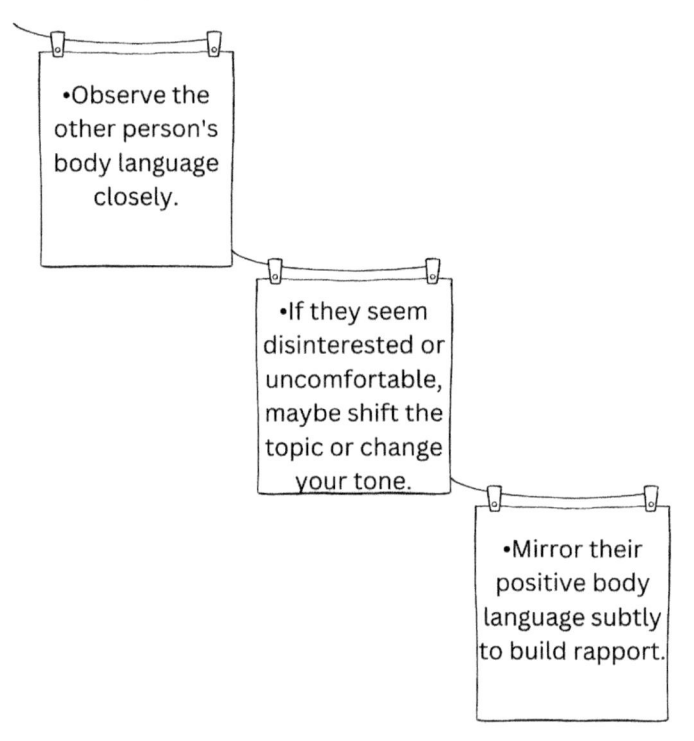

- Observe the other person's body language closely.
- If they seem disinterested or uncomfortable, maybe shift the topic or change your tone.
- Mirror their positive body language subtly to build rapport.

Quick adjustments like these can help turn a "No" into a "Yes." To wrap it up, mastering non-verbal communication can massively improve how accurately and effectively you convey your messages. Not only does it make you more persuasive, but it also helps in understanding others better. And let's be real, who doesn't want to level up their social game?

Remember, communication isn't just about talking; it's about connecting. So next time you're chatting, whether it's with friends, family, or even that girl you've had a crush on since sixth grade, keep an eye on those non-verbal cues. They might just be the secret ingredient to making your conversations truly memorable.

Handling Disputes Positively through Conflict Resolution Techniques

Strong communication skills are absolutely essential for successful relationships and personal growth in teenage boys. Learning to handle disputes and disagreements positively can save you a whole lot of headaches later on. So, let's look into some conflict resolution techniques that will help you navigate tricky conversations with ease and come out stronger on the other side.

First up, active listening and empathy. Envision this: you're having an argument with a friend about whether to play a game of basketball or play video games. Instead of just thinking about your turn, try to really listen to what your friend is saying. Active listening means you give them your full attention, nod when appropriate, and resist the urge to interrupt. By doing this, you'll understand their perspective better, which could be something as simple as "I've had a rough day and need to unwind." Empathy, or putting yourself in their shoes, can go a long way in defusing tension. When both sides feel heard and understood, solving the problem becomes a lot easier (Middle Earth, 2019).

Now, let's talk about collaborative problem-solving. I know it sounds like a mouthful, but it's really about working together to find solutions where everyone benefits. Imagine if instead of fighting over the remote, you and your sibling decided to take turns or watch something you both enjoy.

Here's how you can approach it:

- Start by proposing that you work together to solve the issue.

- Suggest brainstorming ideas, making it clear that everyone's input is valued.
- Evaluate the proposed solutions together and pick the one that seems fair to everyone involved.
- Finally, agree on this solution and stick to it.

By focusing on the problem rather than the people involved, you can come up with a win-win outcome. This makes it less about winning an argument and more about finding a solution that works for everyone (DBT, 2022).

Next, using "I" statements instead of blaming others can be a game-changer. Let's say your friends left you out of a group hangout. Instead of saying, "You guys never include me," you could frame it as, "I felt sad when I wasn't included in the outing." This way, you're expressing your feelings without pointing fingers. It keeps the conversation open and less confrontational. When you avoid blame, people are more likely to listen to what you're saying instead of getting defensive. It's a small change in how you speak, but it has a huge impact on the conversation's outcome.

Moving on to seeking common ground and compromising when necessary. Imagine you and a classmate are assigned a project but have completely different ideas on how to tackle it. Instead of digging your heels in, try to find areas where your ideas overlap. Maybe you both want to create a visually engaging presentation but disagree on the content. You could decide to combine elements from both approaches to make the project even better. Here's what you can do:

- Start by identifying shared goals or interests.

- Openly discuss the points where you disagree and why.
- Look for compromise solutions that incorporate aspects of both viewpoints.
- Agree to meet in the middle if necessary, ensuring that it's a give-and-take situation.

This way, no one feels like they're losing out entirely, and you end up with a solution that at least partly satisfies everyone (DBT, 2022).

So, what's the takeaway? Mastering these conflict resolution skills can help you manage disagreements respectfully and constructively. Strong communication skills aren't just helpful—they're essential. They'll make your relationships smoother and leave you feeling more in control, even in the most heated debates.

One final piece of advice—practice makes perfect. The more you engage in active listening, collaborative problem-solving, and using "I" statements, the better you'll get at it. These skills don't just appear overnight; they need time to develop. Before you know it, you'll be handling conflicts like a pro, improving your relationships, and growing as a person along the way.

In life, disputes and disagreements are going to pop up whether we like it or not. But now, armed with these strategies, you'll be well-prepared to handle them positively. So, go out there and give it a shot. You'd be surprised at how much smoother things can go when you focus on understanding, compromise, and mutual respect. And remember, every challenge is a chance to grow.

CHAPTER 6

Decision Making and Problem-Solving Skills

~

Critical Thinking and Problem-Solving Skills

Think of yourself as an explorer charting new territories. You won't be trekking through jungles or scaling mountains, but it's just as exciting! Consider critical thinking and problem-solving as your navigational tools. They help you find your way through the maze of decisions—whether it's choosing between binge-watching the latest series or preparing for an exam, or deciding if you should join the basketball team or focus on your grades. With these skills in your backpack, you can turn those 'what do I do now?' moments into confident decisions.

Now let's face it: adolescence is like a video game level set to "Extreme." Every day throws new challenges at you—social, academic, or personal—and making the right choice isn't always clear-cut. Imagine you're invited to two events happening at the same time, both equally appealing. Do you go to your best friend's birthday party or attend that school event you've been looking forward to? Or think about a more complex scenario: you're tempted to skip studying for a big test to hang out with friends because, let's be real, fun sounds way better than books. Without critical thinking skills, you might lean towards instant gratification, only to regret it later when faced with consequences like a poor grade.

So what's our game plan for this chapter? We're going to break down how you can analyze situations to make thoughtful decisions. We'll look at evaluating potential outcomes, understanding short- and long- term consequences, and identifying risks and benefits. You'll learn to slice problems into manageable pieces, brainstorm creative solutions, and even embrace trial and error. By the end of this chapter, you'll have a toolkit full of techniques to turn you into a decision-making maestro. Ready to unlock those superpowers? Let's dive in!

Analyzing Situations for Thoughtful Decision-Making

Imagine you've just turned sixteen, and the world feels like it's bursting with opportunities and choices. Do I get a summer job or hang out with friends? Should I try out for the football team or focus on my grades? Choices are everywhere, and they can be tricky to navigate. What if I told you that taking a moment to analyze your options before making a decision could make all the difference? Trust me, it's worth the effort.

Let's start with evaluating potential outcomes. Imagine you're deciding whether to study for an important exam or binge-watch that new show everyone's talking about. It's tempting, right? But here's where we dive in: Before diving into those episodes, consider what happens if you choose to study. Ace the exam, impress your teachers, maybe even unlock some future opportunities. Now, what if you don't study? Sure, you might enjoy the show, but that low grade might not feel so great afterward. Here's what you can do:

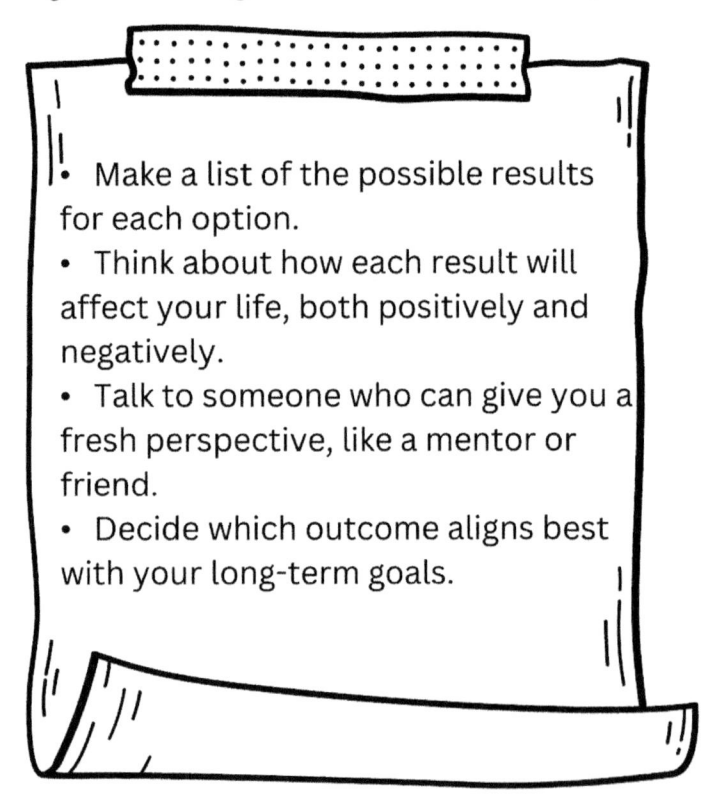

- Make a list of the possible results for each option.
- Think about how each result will affect your life, both positively and negatively.
- Talk to someone who can give you a fresh perspective, like a mentor or friend.
- Decide which outcome aligns best with your long-term goals.

By evaluating these outcomes, you're already a step ahead in mastering the art of decision-making (Elwyn et al., 2010). It's like having a superpower that prevents you from being swayed by short-term temptations. Cool, right?

Now, let's tackle understanding the importance of considering short-term and long-term consequences. Picture this: You're at a party, and someone offers you a drink. In the short term, you might think, "Why not? Everyone's doing it." But hold up—what about the long-term effects? You could end up in trouble with your parents, or worse, face legal issues. Here's a tip: Before you make any snap decisions, stop and think beyond the immediate moment.

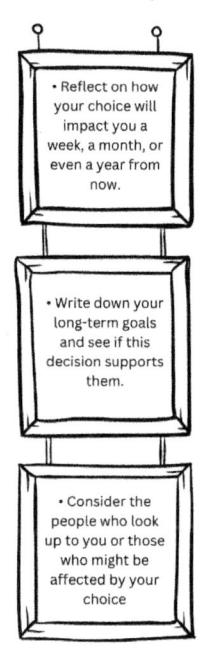

- Reflect on how your choice will impact you a week, a month, or even a year from now.

- Write down your long-term goals and see if this decision supports them.

- Consider the people who look up to you or those who might be affected by your choice

Seeing the bigger picture helps steer your ship in the right direction, avoiding rocky paths and stormy waters (Dartmouth, n.d.). You're not just living for the moment; you're crafting your future. How awesome is that?

Next up is learning to identify possible risks and benefits associated with each decision. Let's say you're thinking about investing your hard-earned money into a cool gadget or saving it for something more substantial, like a car. What are the risks and benefits?

- Research each option thoroughly.

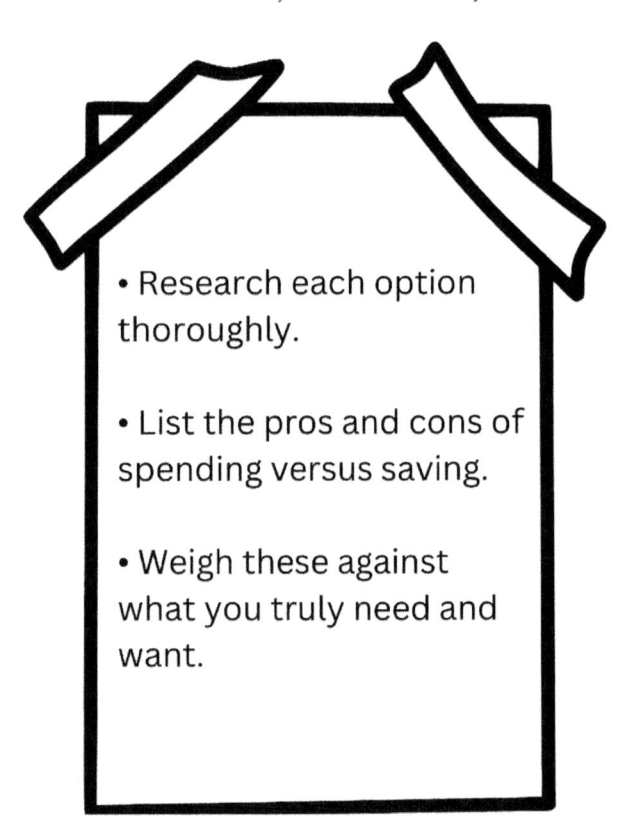

- List the pros and cons of spending versus saving.

- Weigh these against what you truly need and want.

By breaking it down, you can identify hidden pitfalls or unexpected advantages. Maybe that car not only gets you around but also opens up job opportunities. On the flip side, the cool gadget might lose its appeal after a while. Identifying risks and benefits keeps you grounded and helps make informed choices.

Finally, when it comes to enhancing your analytical skills and critical thinking, practice makes perfect. Just like you wouldn't expect to ace a free-throw on your first try, you shouldn't expect to be a decision- making master overnight. Start small. Run through different scenarios in your head or even play decision-making games. Here's how you can sharpen those skills:

- Create hypothetical situations and decide what you would do in each case.
- Discuss these scenarios with friends and family, getting their input and perspectives.
- Keep a journal of your daily decisions to track the outcomes and learn from them.
- Engage in activities that challenge your thinking, such as puzzles or strategic games.

Practicing these scenarios and stretching your mental muscles is like training for a marathon. Over time, it becomes second nature, and making thoughtful decisions won't seem so daunting anymore.

To sum it all up, analyzing situations before acting can prevent impulsive decisions and lead to better outcomes. By evaluating potential outcomes, considering short- and long-term consequences, identifying risks and benefits, and practicing decision-making scenarios, you're building a strong foundation for making wise choices. Remember, every decision shapes your journey, and being equipped with critical thinking and problem-solving skills empowers you to steer your own course confidently.

So next time you're faced with a decision, take a moment, breathe, and think it through. Whether it's choosing between soccer practice or game night, or deciding to save up or splurge, a bit of reflection can turn a quick decision into a powerful one.

Equipping with Problem- Solving Techniques

One of the most critical skills a teenage boy can develop is the ability to solve problems effectively. Imagine you're stuck on a level in your favorite video game. You wouldn't keep trying the same failed strategy, would you? Nope, you'd try something new, break it down into more manageable steps, or even look at hints and tips online. The same approach applies to real-life problems—breaking them down into smaller parts makes them far less overwhelming.

First off, let's talk about breaking down those big, hairy problems. Think of a complex issue like a giant pizza. Trying to eat it all in one go would be impossible (and gross). But slice it up, and suddenly, it's no big deal. When you face a tough problem, start by identifying its different components. For instance, if you're struggling with math homework, pinpoint whether it's an issue understanding the instructions, the formulas, or maybe the entire topic itself. Each part is more manageable separately, just like those pizza slices.

Breaking big problems into smaller bits accomplishes three key things:

- It reduces anxiety, making the problem seem less intimidating.

- It allows for focus on one piece at a time, which is much easier than tackling everything at once.

- It helps track progress as each piece gets solved, boosting your confidence along the way.

Now, onto brainstorming—a tool that transforms chaos into creativity. Picture this: You're in a room with friends, and someone suggests the most absurd idea you've ever heard. Instead of laughing it off, the idea snowballs into something genius. Brainstorming works similarly. Gather a notebook or open a blank document on your phone. Start jotting down every potential solution, no matter how outlandish. This isn't the time for self-censorship; crazy ideas often lead to brilliant solutions. Here's how you can make brainstorming effective:

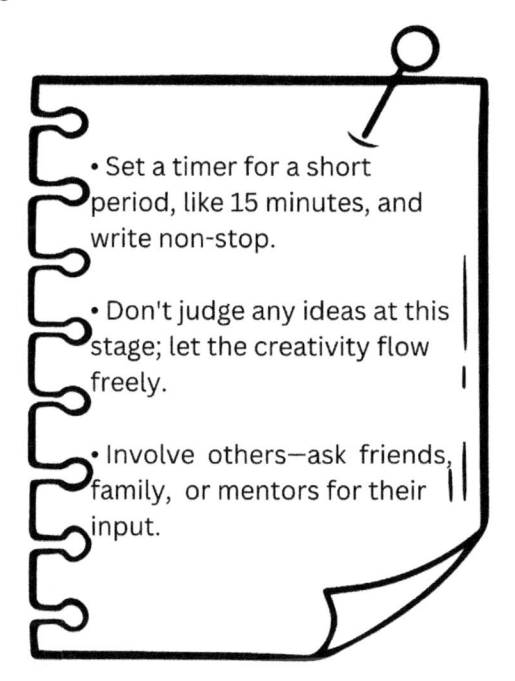

- Set a timer for a short period, like 15 minutes, and write non-stop.

- Don't judge any ideas at this stage; let the creativity flow freely.

- Involve others—ask friends, family, or mentors for their input.

The beauty of brainstorming is its spontaneity and unpredictability. By pooling together a variety of ideas, you're likely to stumble upon innovative solutions you'd never think of while sitting alone in a quiet room, overthinking.

Next, let's embrace the good old trial-and-error method. Remember when you first learned to ride a bike? Wobbling, falling, getting back up—that's trial and error in action. Solving problems can often feel the same way. You won't always get it right on the first try, and that's perfectly okay. The goal is to test various solutions and learn from the results.

> **To get the most out of trial and error:**
>
> • Treat failures as valuable feedback rather than setbacks.
>
> • Keep track of what works and what doesn't, so you don't repeat the same mistakes.
>
> • Be persistent. Effective solutions sometimes come after many attempts.

For example, say you're trying to improve your performance in a sport. Try different training regimens, diets, and routines. Document the outcomes meticulously. Eventually, you'll find the combination that works best for you. Success comes not from getting it right immediately but from continuously refining your approach based on real- world results.

Lastly, don't be shy about seeking advice. Sometimes, the best solutions come from a fresh perspective. Think about it: When you're struggling with a tough play in a game, you'd probably consult your coach or ask a more experienced teammate for help. Life isn't much different. Reaching out to peers or mentors when you're stumped can provide insights you might have missed.

When asking for feedback or advice:

- Choose individuals who have relevant experience or expertise.

- Be specific about the problem you're facing, so they know exactly how to help.

- Listen actively and consider their suggestions, even if they initially seem counterintuitive.

Seeking advice shows maturity and a willingness to grow. It's a sign of strength, not weakness. Plus, you'll build a network of people you can rely on when things get tough, which is invaluable.

The key takeaway here is simple yet powerful: Problem-solving skills enable you to approach challenges with a structured mindset and persistence. With these techniques—breaking down problems into smaller parts, brainstorming, using trial and error, and seeking advice—you'll develop a robust toolkit to handle anything life throws your way. Not only will you be more equipped to tackle your current issues, but you'll also set yourself up for future success. So, next time you're faced with a seemingly insurmountable challenge, remember that it's just another pizza waiting to be sliced, one piece at a time.Learning from Failures and Setbacks

Failures. Nobody likes them, but let's face it: they're an inevitable part of life. You spill that soda on your new sneakers, flunk a math test because you forgot to study (again), or you get benched in the big game after missing an easy goal. These experiences can sting, sure, but they also offer invaluable lessons if you're open to learning from them.

Embracing failure as a learning opportunity rather than a defeat is crucial. Picture this: you've just bombed a science project presentation. Instead of thinking, "I'm the worst at this," consider asking yourself, "What went wrong, and how can I improve?"

Here are some simple steps to guide you through:

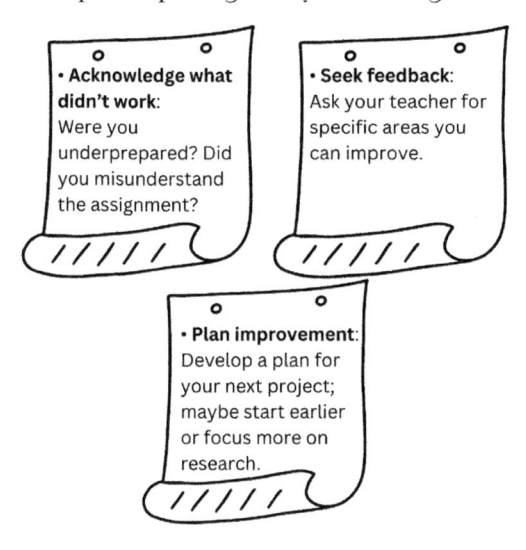

- **Acknowledge what didn't work**: Were you underprepared? Did you misunderstand the assignment?

- **Seek feedback**: Ask your teacher for specific areas you can improve.

- **Plan improvement**: Develop a plan for your next project; maybe start earlier or focus more on research.

Reflecting on past mistakes to identify areas for improvement in decision-making is another critical skill. Think back to your science project fiasco. Maybe you realize you procrastinated too much. Reflecting involves a bit of self-analysis.

Here's what you can do:

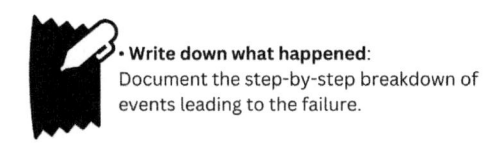

- **Write down what happened**: Document the step-by-step breakdown of events leading to the failure.

- **Analyze**: Identify the key mistakes and think about what you could have done differently.

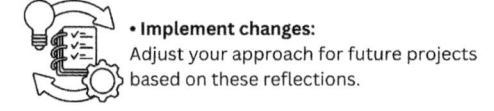

- **Implement changes**: Adjust your approach for future projects based on these reflections.

Remember that setbacks are a natural part of growth and development. Take Michael Jordan, for instance- cut from his high school basketball team but now known as one of the greatest athletes ever. Each misstep was a setup for his incredible leap forward.

Setbacks should be seen not as signs of incompetence but as golden opportunities to grow stronger and wiser.

Developing a positive mindset that views challenges as stepping stones to success is also vital. Imagine you're climbing a steep hill. It's tough, tiring, and sometimes you slip. But each step brings you closer to the summit and builds your leg muscles. Similarly, every challenge you face strengthens your problem- solving skills and resilience.

Teenage years often feel like a whirlwind of emotions, decisions, and unforeseen obstacles. Sometimes it seems like everything is going wrong all at once. But what if we embraced these moments instead of fearing them?

Take Eric. He was an average teenager with dreams of coding the next Minecraft. One day, he decided to create his own video game as a summer project. He poured hours into it, only to find out the code he wrote was full of bugs. Instead of letting frustration take over, Eric saw this failure as an opportunity. He sought help, joined online forums, and learned from his mistakes. By the end of the summer, he had created a functional game, albeit a simple one. The point? The initial failure didn't deter him; it set him on a path of continuous improvement and learning.

When you encounter failures, remember that resilience isn't some magical trait reserved for superheroes. It's built through behaviors, thoughts, and actions that anyone can develop (First Coast YMCA,

2024). Resilience means bouncing back from adversity, whether it's failing a test or getting rejected by a crush. It involves facing these difficulties head-on, learning from them, and moving forward.

Here's another example: Lucas wanted to join the track team. He practiced daily but still didn't make the cut during tryouts. Instead of giving up, he approached his coach for tips and guidance. Over the next few months, Lucas worked on his weaknesses, participated in local races, and improved significantly. When the next tryouts came around, he made the team. This journey highlighted the power of persistence and learning from setbacks.

Adopting a mindset where failure is a strategic component of success can transform your outlook. As in entrepreneurship, understanding that failure is an integral part of the journey can lead to significant personal growth (Marketing, 2024). Think of each setback as a minor detour rather than a dead-end.

Remember, failure is a common factor in many aspects of life, including the startup world. Entrepreneurs who adopt a "failing forward" mindset see each failure as a stepping stone toward eventual success. They embrace a growth mindset, learn from mistakes, and build resilience—traits that are equally valuable for students (Wadhwani Foundation, 2024).

To wrap it up, here's a quick recap:

- Embrace failure as an opportunity to learn rather than a definitive defeat. Understand that making mistakes is part of the growth process.
- Reflect on past mistakes to pinpoint areas for improvement. This helps refine your decision-making skills over time.

- Recognize that setbacks are just bumps along the road to success. They don't define you but shape you into a more resilient individual.
- Foster a positive mindset that looks at challenges as necessary steps in your journey toward achieving your goals.

Building resilience and developing critical thinking and problem-solving abilities begins with changing how you react to failure. So next time you stumble, view it as a chance to stand up stronger and smarter. Failure isn't the opposite of success; it's a crucial part of the journey there.

Seeking Guidance and Support

Recognizing when expert opinion or guidance can provide clarity in decision-making processes is like having a secret weapon in the world of teenage dilemmas. Imagine you're trying to figure out if you should take that advanced math class, join the basketball team, or maybe even decide whether pineapple belongs on pizza (spoiler: it does). Sometimes, it feels like you're stuck in a maze with no exit. But here's where the magic happens: seeking advice from someone who knows more than you can be your map out of confusion.

So how do you know when it's time to call in the pros? Picture this: You're knee-deep in a science project but can't tell a hypothesis from a conclusion. That's a solid clue to seek help. Got a tricky situation with friends or deciding what college courses to pick? Look for experts - your teachers, mentors, or even that wise uncle everyone secretly goes to for advice.

Here's what you can do in order to achieve the goal:

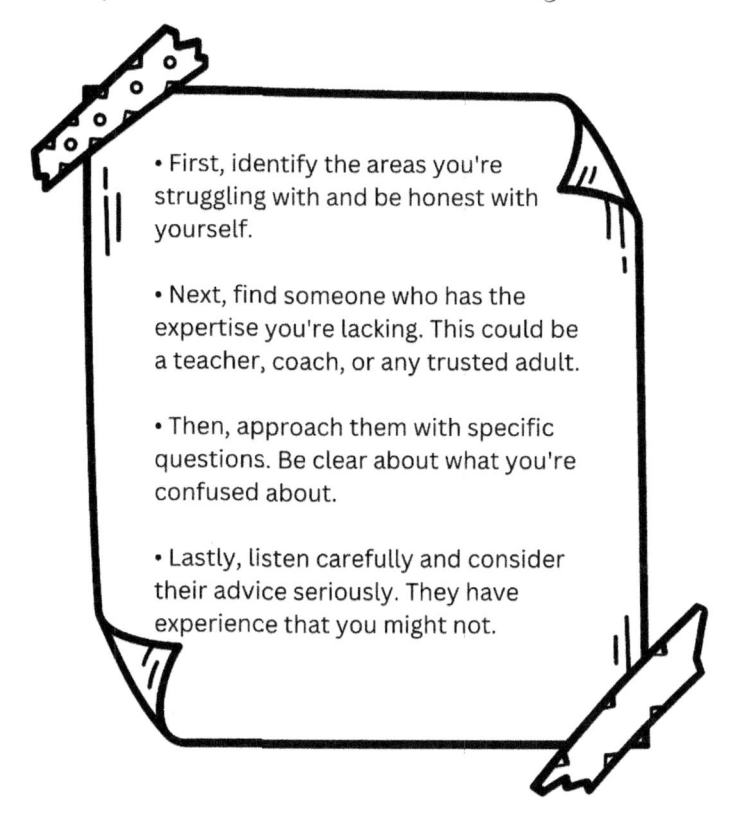

- First, identify the areas you're struggling with and be honest with yourself.

- Next, find someone who has the expertise you're lacking. This could be a teacher, coach, or any trusted adult.

- Then, approach them with specific questions. Be clear about what you're confused about.

- Lastly, listen carefully and consider their advice seriously. They have experience that you might not.

Now, let's move on to establishing a network of trusted individuals for seeking guidance and advice. Think of this network as your very own Justice League, ready to jump in whenever you need help. The best part? You get to choose who's in it.

Start by picking people who have proven they have your back. Maybe it's your best friend who always gives honest feedback, your parents who've been through similar teenage drama, or your school counselor who seems to have endless wisdom. Diversify your crew with folks from different parts of your life – this way, you'll have someone for every type of crisis. For example, if you're grappling with academic decisions, your teachers and academic advisor are perfect. If it's something more personal, like relationships or emotional support, your close friends and family members can offer comfort and advice. Building these connections early on means you're never truly alone when faced with tough choices.

Being open to different perspectives and feedback when making important decisions is crucial. It's easy to fall into the trap of echo chambers where everyone agrees with you. But imagine trying to solve a Rubik's cube while only looking at one side —you'd be missing the bigger picture.

Here's a fun way to practice this: next time you and your friends debate the best superhero movie, really listen to their arguments. You might think "The Dark Knight" is unmatched, but hearing why someone loves "Black Panther" opens up new angles. Apply this openness to real-life decisions too.

When your mom suggests joining that extracurricular activity you're unsure about, don't just roll your eyes. Consider her reasons. Your friend says you'd make a good team captain? Ask why they think so. Different viewpoints can spotlight aspects you hadn't considered before, making your decision-making more rounded and informed.

Utilizing resources, such as books, online articles, or mentors for additional support is like having an arsenal of tools at your disposal. You wouldn't build a treehouse with just a hammer, right? The same goes for tackling life's challenges.

Books are goldmines of knowledge, offering insights from professionals who've spent years mastering their craft. Whether it's a self-help book on managing stress or a guide on choosing a career path, there's likely something written that's worth your time. Don't underestimate the power of reading – it's like having a lifetime's worth of advice pressed between pages.

Online articles are another fantastic resource. Platforms like Khan Academy can break down complex subjects into digestible pieces. Websites like Medium host a plethora of personal experiences and professional advice columns that could resonate with your situation. Just be sure to verify the credibility of your sources; stick to well-known sites and authors with credentials that match the advice they're giving. And never forget the most invaluable resource – mentors. These are people who've walked the path you're on and can provide tailored, experienced- based guidance. NASA's DEVELOP Program is one such avenue where young minds collaborate with seasoned professionals to tackle real-world problems using Earth observation data (Friedl et al., n.d.).

So what's the end-game here? Seeking guidance doesn't mean you're incapable; it signifies maturity and a willingness to learn. It leads to more informed decisions and broadens your perspective on problem-solving. Plus, it's pretty cool to tap into the brains of those who've already navigated through the minefield you're entering.

In essence, life throws curveballs, but you don't have to catch them alone. By recognizing when to seek expert opinion, building a network of trusted advisers, embracing different perspectives, and utilizing available resources, you're setting yourself up for smarter decisions and fewer regrets. And remember, it's okay to ask for directions when you're lost – it just might lead you to places you never imagined!

As you continue on this journey, keep in mind that every choice counts and each moment of thoughtfulness brings you closer to mastering your path. Cheers to making those smart choices, one thoughtful decision at a time!

CHAPTER 7

Understanding and Managing Emotions

Developing Emotional Intelligence

Imagine for a moment you're on a roller coaster that jerks you up and then plunges you down, spins you around until you're dizzy, and leaves you gasping for air. That, my friends, is what teenage emotions feel like. One minute you're king of the world because you aced a test, the next you're convinced your life is over because you missed an easy shot. It's wild, unpredictable, and it can feel downright impossible to navigate. But guess what? Developing emotional intelligence is like strapping on a seatbelt—firmly keeping you in place no matter how topsy-turvy the ride gets.

So, what's the deal with this emotional roller coaster anyway? Let's break it down. Maybe you've noticed that sometimes when you're angry, it's not just anger bubbling under the surface. Perhaps there's a cocktail of sadness, disappointment, or even fear mixed in there too. Take that time when your friend canceled plans last minute. Sure, you were mad, but wasn't there also a hint of loneliness creeping in? Or how about when you crushed it in a basketball game but still felt inexplicably bummed out afterward? These mixed-up emotions are confusing, right? Without understanding them, you might end up yelling at your friend or sulking in your room alone, feeling even worse.

Now here's where things get interesting. In this chapter, we're diving into the nitty-gritty of developing emotional intelligence. That means you'll learn how to spot your emotions, label them like a pro, and understand where they're coming from. We'll kick things off with some practical exercises to help you get in touch with your feelings, like journaling your daily experiences and triggers. Then, we'll talk about the importance of open discussions with friends or mentors about what you're going through emotionally. By the end, you'll have a toolkit full of strategies to help you master your emotional landscape, making life's challenges feel less like terrifying free falls and more like exciting loops on an epic adventure ride.

Enhancing Emotional Awareness

Recognizing and labeling emotions can sometimes feel like trying to catch a cloud with your bare hands. But trust me, it's possible—and incredibly important for building the kind of emotional intelligence that helps you navigate life's ups and downs. Imagine how different the world would be if we all had a better grip on our own feelings. Let's dive into some ideas on how to get started.

First, let's talk about the importance of teaching you how to identify and label your emotions accurately. It might sound basic, but it's surprisingly easy to confuse feelings like anger, sadness, and joy. Take anger, for instance. It's more than just rage; it could be masking fear or disappointment. Recognizing this difference is crucial. For example, imagine you're mad at a friend for canceling plans. Is it pure anger, or is it also a twinge of sadness because you were looking forward to hanging out? Knowing the difference changes the way you address the situation. You see, understanding your emotional landscape isn't just a touchy-feely exercise; it's a roadmap to better decisions and relationships.

Now, let's kick things up a notch with practical exercises for emotional recognition and self-reflection. This is where the rubber meets the road. One effective method is journaling. Set aside a few minutes each day to jot down what you felt throughout the day and what triggered those emotions. Was it something someone said? A specific event? Even honing in on seemingly minor triggers can reveal patterns over time.

Here's what you can do:

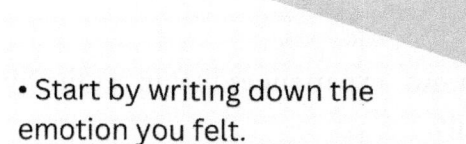

- Start by writing down the emotion you felt.

- Next, describe the situation that led to that feeling.

- Reflect on why you think you reacted that way.

- Lastly, consider whether your reaction was helpful or if there's a better way you could handle similar situations in the future.

Through this daily practice, you'll start to notice trends and triggers, giving you the power to predict and manage your reactions better. Think of it as emotional muscle memory!

Another powerful tool is open discussions about emotions within peer groups or with a trusted mentor. Let's face it, talking about feelings might seem awkward, especially for teenage boys. But normalizing these conversations can break down barriers and make emotional awareness second nature. Find a group of friends or a mentor who's willing to take the plunge and talk about what they're feeling openly.

Here's how to get started:

- Begin the conversation with a simple prompt like, "What's something that made you really happy or upset recently?"
- Share your own experiences first to set the tone and show vulnerability.

Encourage everyone to use "I" statements, focusing on their own feelings rather than passing judgment. These conversations are not just about airing grievances; they're about understanding that everyone goes through similar emotional journeys. The more you talk, the easier it gets, and soon enough, discussing emotions won't seem like such a big deal. Plus, you'll find that it strengthens your friendships and provides an invaluable support network.

Introducing the concept of emotional intelligence and its importance is a game changer. Emotional intelligence—or EQ—is essentially the ability to understand and manage your own emotions while also recognizing and influencing the emotions of others. Why does this matter? Because high EQ translates to better leadership, stronger relationships, and even improved academic performance (GreatSchools, 2021). When you can read a room and empathize with others, you're in a much better position to navigate complex social situations and make sound decisions.

Now, let's bring it full circle. Improved emotional vocabulary and awareness lead to better self- regulation and communication skills. Imagine being able to articulate exactly why you're upset instead of just lashing out. Picture yourself calming down during a heated moment because you recognize the underlying emotion and know it'll pass. Or think about how much smoother relationships would be if everyone could clearly express their needs and fears.

So, next time you feel a surge of emotions coming on, don't just ride the wave—analyze it, name it, and share it. With a little practice, you'll be well on your way to mastering your emotional landscape, building resilience, and overcoming challenges with grace. And if you're ever in doubt, remember: developing emotional intelligence is not a destination but a journey, one that makes life's roller coaster a lot less daunting and a lot more manageable.

Managing Stress and Anxiety

Let's face it: navigating the teenage years can sometimes feel like fighting a dragon with nothing but a paper sword. The pressures of school, social life, and maybe even some family stuff sneak up on you, leading to stress and anxiety that seem impossible to conquer. But what if I told you that developing emotional intelligence, beginning with practical techniques to manage stress and anxiety, is the key to not only overcoming these challenges but building resilience too? It's all about learning how to handle life's curveballs with poise.

First, let's talk about relaxation techniques. You've probably heard the term "mindfulness" thrown around quite a bit. Sounds kinda fluffy, right? But mindfulness meditation and deep breathing exercises are like secret weapons against stress. Picture this: You've just got a ton of homework, your phone's buzzing non-stop, and you're feeling the walls closing in.

Here's what you can do:

- **Find a quiet spot.** No phones allowed.

- **Sit comfortably** and close your eyes.

- **Take a deep breath in,** hold it for a second, and then slowly breathe out. Repeat this a few times.

- **Focus on your breath.** Notice the sensation of the air coming in and out. If your mind wanders (and it will), gently bring your focus back to your breathing.

It sounds simple, but trust me, it's powerful. Research shows that practices like these can significantly reduce stress levels and boost overall well-being (How to help children and teens manage their stress, n.d.). Plus, doing this regularly helps train your brain to stay calm even when life gets chaotic.

Now, let's dive into strategies for addressing specific stressors. Academic pressure is a big one. We've all been there—staring at a mountain of assignments, feeling paralyzed by deadlines. Time management can be your best friend here.

Start by:

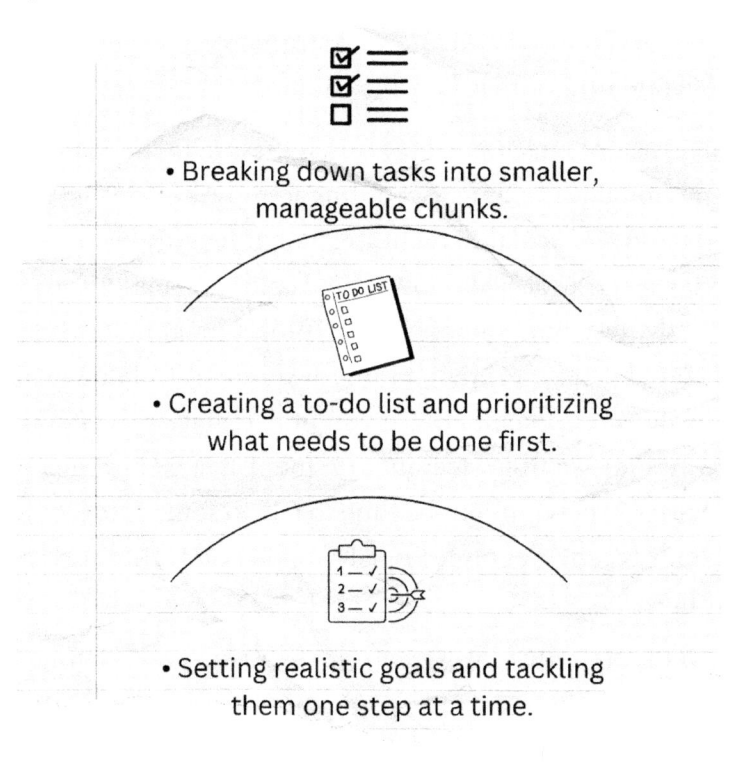

- Breaking down tasks into smaller, manageable chunks.

- Creating a to-do list and prioritizing what needs to be done first.

- Setting realistic goals and tackling them one step at a time.

Another common stressor is social anxiety. Maybe you're nervous about speaking in class or meeting new people. A good technique here is to rehearse and practice these situations. Try talking in front of a mirror or role-playing with a friend. And remember, it's okay to start small. Complimenting someone on their shoes or joining a club where you share common interests can gradually build your confidence.

Here's another game-changer: engaging in physical activities and hobbies. Staying active isn't just about building muscles or training for a marathon; it's an excellent way to blow off steam. Regular exercise releases endorphins—the ultimate mood lifters. Whether it's shooting hoops, skateboarding, or just taking a brisk walk in the park, find something you enjoy. Adding a creative hobby can also be a lifesaver. Drawing, playing an instrument, or even cooking can serve as wonderful outlets for your emotions.

A lot of teens underestimate how much these activities can improve their emotional well-being. According to the APA, getting involved in sports and pro-social activities can significantly decrease stress and foster a sense of accomplishment and camaraderie (AACAP, n.d.). Lastly, let's touch upon seeking professional help when stress and anxiety become overwhelming. It's crucial to know when it's time to call in reinforcements. If you notice that stress is impacting your daily life—trouble sleeping, frequent headaches, changes in eating habits, etc.—it might be time to talk to someone. Counselors and therapists can offer professional support and techniques tailored to your needs.

One real-life story that sticks with me involves a teen named Max. Max was always the life of the party, but underneath, he struggled with anxiety and academic pressure. He started seeing a school counselor who helped him adopt relaxation techniques and better time management skills.

Slowly but surely, Max saw improvements not only in his grades but in his overall happiness. This isn't just a fairy tale; it's what happens when you take proactive steps towards managing stress. Everyone's journey is different, but everyone has the capacity to develop emotional intelligence and resilience.

In short, practical stress management tools are more than just survival tactics—they empower you. They give you the upper hand when facing daily pressures and challenges. Equipping yourself with these skills doesn't mean you'll never experience stress again—let's be real, life is full of unexpected twists and turns—but it means you'll be prepared to handle whatever comes your way with confidence and grace. By embracing these techniques, you're not only managing stress but building a foundation for a resilient future. So the next time life hands you a lemon, you won't just make lemonade; you'll add a splash of pizzazz and turn it into a deliciously refreshing drink that keeps you cool under pressure.

Healthy Coping Mechanisms

Let's dive into something crucial yet often overlooked: developing healthy coping mechanisms for emotional challenges. When emotions run high, having reliable methods to cope is a game-changer. Let's explore how journaling, creative expression, and physical activity can help you navigate emotional ups and downs.

During emotionally challenging times, journaling can be your best buddy. Think of it as having a conversation with yourself. It's like dumping all those nagging thoughts onto paper so they don't clog up your brain. You might start by jotting down whatever comes to mind, no filter needed. Soon enough, patterns will emerge, shedding light on what's truly bugging you (Healthy Coping Strategies for Kids and Teens, n.d.).

Creative expression is another fantastic outlet. Whether you're sketching, painting, sculpting, or even strumming a guitar, these activities allow you to externalize feelings that words can't capture.

Plus, there's something incredibly satisfying about turning raw emotion into art. It's like your very own superpower—transforming stress into something beautiful.

Don't forget physical activity. Exercise isn't just about getting ripped; it's also a proven mood-lifter. A quick jog, a basketball game, or even a fast-paced walk releases endorphins—a.k.a. the "happy hormones." These activities help burn off frustration and give you a break from overthinking.

Next, let's talk about the difference between adaptive and maladaptive coping mechanisms without sounding too text-bookish.

Adaptive coping mechanisms are like the good guys in a superhero movie. They help you handle stress in ways that build you up rather than tear you down. Seeking support from friends or family, taking time for self-care, and solving problems step-by-step are classic examples. On the other hand, we've got maladaptive coping mechanisms—think of them as the villains. These tactics might offer immediate relief but can wreak havoc long-term. Substance abuse, avoidance behaviors, or lashing out in anger fall into this category. Now for some guidelines: if you're feeling overwhelmed and need a healthier direction, consider these steps:

- Start by writing down what's bothering you.

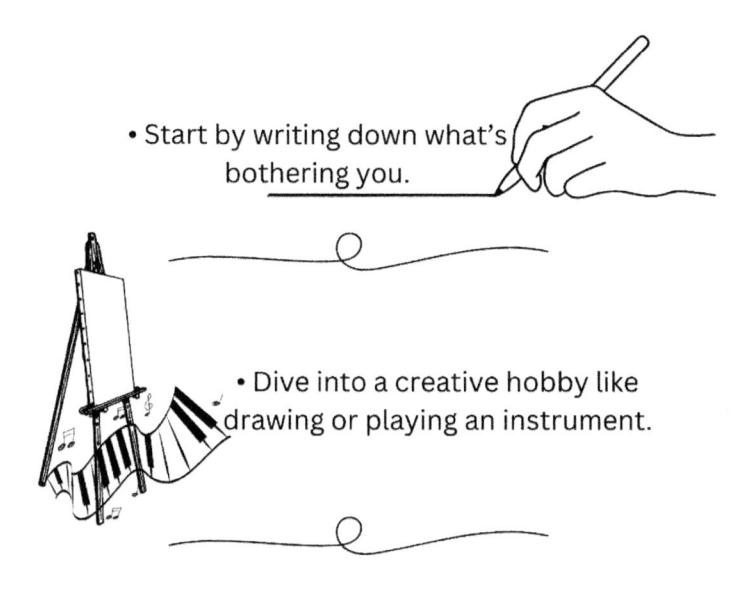

- Dive into a creative hobby like drawing or playing an instrument.

- Get moving with some exercise to shake off the funk.

Setting boundaries is equally important. Knowing your limits and communicating them helps maintain emotional balance. If you're not comfortable doing something, speak up. Establishing personal space protects your mental health and fosters respect in relationships.

To incorporate these habits:

- Schedule time each day solely for things you love.

- Practice saying "No" politely but firmly when you're stretched thin.

- Remember, it's perfectly okay to prioritize your needs occasionally.

Finally, let's delve into self-compassion and accepting emotions without judgment. Imagine treating yourself like you would your best friend. You wouldn't harshly criticize them for feeling down, right? So why do it to yourself? Self-compassion involves acknowledging your emotions as valid and understanding that everyone has rough patches.

Accepting emotions without judgment means recognizing feelings without smothering them with negativity. Instead of labeling emotions as "good" or "bad," see them as signals offering insight into what's happening inside you. This mindset shift can transform how you deal with emotional challenges.

In essence, consider adopting habits that foster a kinder internal dialogue:

- Next time you mess up, remind yourself that everyone makes mistakes.

- When a negative emotion arises, observe it without labeling or dramatizing.

- Reflect on past experiences where you've overcome difficulties—this reinforces resilience and self-kindness.

So, what's the bottom line? Building a toolbox of healthy coping skills enhances emotional well-being and fosters resilience. Start small—with journaling, a bit of creative work, or a daily jog.

Gradually, incorporate self-care routines and set boundaries to protect your emotional space. Above all, practice self-compassion. Accepting your emotions without judgment opens the door to growth and resilience. By equipping yourself with these tools, you'll be better prepared to face life's challenges head-on.

Remember, it's not just about surviving tough times but thriving despite them. Developing emotional intelligence through these strategies arms you with the resilience needed to bounce back stronger, every single time. So next time, instead of bottling up your feelings or resorting to negative behaviors, reach into your toolbox of healthy coping mechanisms. You've got this!

By embracing these methods, you invest in a future where emotional challenges become opportunities for growth. Becoming more emotionally intelligent doesn't just benefit you—it positively impacts everyone around you. So why not start today? Each step you take brings you closer to mastering the art of resilience and building a happier, healthier life.

Mindfulness Practices

Developing emotional intelligence is a key step in overcoming life's challenges and building resilience. Imagine being able to handle stress like a pro, focusing more clearly on homework, and reacting less when things don't go your way. Sounds pretty great, right? Let's talk about how you can achieve this through mindfulness practices.

Mindfulness might seem like one of those adult buzzwords, often thrown around in yoga classes or health magazines, but it's actually a super useful tool for reducing stress, improving concentration, and regulating emotions. Think of it as a brain workout, kind of like lifting weights, but for your mind.

Mindfulness is all about paying attention to the present moment without judgment. When you're mindful, you engage fully with whatever you're doing. Whether it's eating, walking, or even breathing, mindfulness allows you to experience these activities deeply. Studies have shown that practicing mindfulness regularly can help reduce the production of stress hormones, boost immune function, and improve sleep quality (camptuku, 2023). Plus, it makes you feel good. Who wouldn't want that?

To get started, let's try some basic mindfulness exercises. You don't need any fancy equipment, just yourself and a little bit of time.

First up is the body scan. Sit or lie down somewhere comfortable and close your eyes. Slowly bring your attention to different parts of your body, starting from your toes and moving up to your head. Notice any sensations, tension, or discomfort without trying to change anything. It's like giving yourself a mini check-up. If your mind starts to wander—which it inevitably will—gently bring your focus back to your body. This exercise helps you become more attuned to what you're feeling physically, which can help you respond better to stress.

Next, try mindful breathing. Find a quiet spot where you won't be disturbed. Sit comfortably with your back straight, and close your eyes if that feels okay. Pay attention to your breath as it goes in and out. Notice the rise and fall of your chest or the sensation of air flowing through your nostrils. If your mind starts to race, that's perfectly normal. Just gently guide it back to your breath. Even just a few minutes of this can make you feel more centered and calm.

Another cool technique is sensory awareness. Pick an object—let's say an apple. Look at it closely. Notice its color, texture, and shape. Then, take a bite and focus on the taste, smell, and the sound it makes as you chew. This works well with other activities too, like listening to music or even washing dishes. The idea is to immerse yourself completely in the experience, which can help pull your mind away from worries and stress.

Now, let's integrate mindfulness into your daily routine. One easy way is through mindful eating. Instead of rushing through meals or munching while watching TV, take a moment to really notice the food you're eating. Observe its colors, textures, and flavors. Chew slowly and appreciate every bite. This not only helps you enjoy your food more but also aids digestion and reduces overeating.

You can also practice mindful walking. Whether you're strolling to school, walking the dog, or just pacing in your room, pay attention to each step. Feel the ground under your feet and notice how your body moves. This makes even simple walks more enjoyable and calming.

How about creating a bedtime mindfulness ritual? Before you hit the sack, spend a few minutes focusing on your breath or doing a quick body scan. It helps clear your mind, making it easier to drift off to sleep. Better sleep leads to better mood and improved focus during the day, so everyone wins.

The real beauty of mindfulness lies in its connection to emotional resilience. Life throws curveballs all the time, and being resilient means you're better equipped to handle them without falling apart. Research shows that mindfulness helps in managing emotions by allowing us to observe our thoughts and feelings without getting overwhelmed (Dai et al., 2021/12/12).

Let's look at an example. Suppose you're having a rough day because you flunked a test or had a disagreement with a friend. Instead of letting negative emotions spiral out of control, mindfulness teaches you to acknowledge these feelings without amplifying them. You might think, "I'm feeling disappointed right now," rather than, "I'm such a failure." This subtle shift can make a huge difference in how you cope with tough situations.

Here's what you can do to incorporate mindfulness effectively:

- During meals, focus entirely on your food. Notice the flavors, textures, and smells.
- While walking, pay attention to each step you take and the world around you.
- Set aside a few minutes before bed for some deep breathing or a body scan.
- Make time for short mindfulness sessions throughout your day, even if it's just a minute or two.

Practicing mindfulness isn't just about sitting quietly and meditating; it's a versatile skill you can apply to many aspects of life. By incorporating these practices into your daily routine, you'll be better prepared to face challenges with a clear mind and balanced emotions. In summary, mindfulness isn't just for adults or yogis. It's a practical, science-backed tool that teenage boys can use to improve focus, reduce stress, and build emotional resilience. With a bit of practice, you'll find yourself handling life's ups and downs with a lot more grace and ease. So why not give it a shot? Your mind and body will thank you.

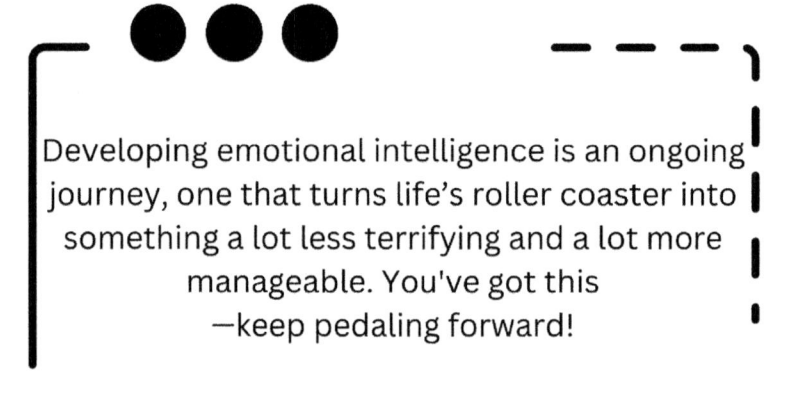

> ● ● ●
>
> Developing emotional intelligence is an ongoing journey, one that turns life's roller coaster into something a lot less terrifying and a lot more manageable. You've got this
> —keep pedaling forward!

CHAPTER 8

Healthy Relationships and Boundaries

Healthy Relationship Dynamics

Imagine you are studying for a crucial exam, and suddenly, your little brother bursts into the room, disrupting your focus. Annoying, isn't it? This simple scenario highlights a more significant concept— setting personal boundaries. Just as you safeguard your study time from distractions, it's essential to protect your emotional well-being from external influence. For teenage boys, grasping the importance of creating and honoring boundaries is as valuable as acing a difficult subject in school.

So, what's the big deal about boundaries anyway? Imagine this: Your friend always makes backhanded comments, disguised as jokes, about your clothes or interests. At first, you might laugh it off, but over time, it starts getting under your skin, right? Or when someone keeps texting you at all hours, completely ignoring that you need some downtime. These are subtle yet clear signs of unhealthy relationships. The problem is, if you don't recognize these red flags, you could end up feeling stressed, anxious, and downright miserable.

Identifying toxic behaviors early on and understanding how they impact you is key to maintaining your mental and emotional health.

In this chapter, we'll tackle everything from spotting toxic relationships to setting firm boundaries with humor and relatable examples. You'll learn how to communicate openly about what's bothering you without starting World War III and get practical tips on asserting your needs confidently. We'll also discuss why trusting your gut is as crucial as nailing a perfect shot in basketball and how talking to trusted adults can feel like gaining a valuable playbook.

> Ready to transform your relationships and boost your emotional well-being? Let's dive in and get started!

Identifying Toxic Relationships and Developing Boundaries

Recognizing signs of toxicity in relationships can be a game-changer for your emotional well-being. Visualize the following scenario: You've got a buddy who's always trying to control your every move, from what you wear to whom you hang out with. That is one major red flag! Control and manipulation are classic signs that the relationship isn't healthy. It's like having a personal referee who doesn't let you play the game your way.

But how do you spot the subtle ones? Well, take a moment to look at how your friend communicates. Are they sarcastic all the time and cover it up as "just joking"? Do they blame you for things that go wrong and never take responsibility? This kind of toxic communication can mess with your head big time. Recognizing these behaviors early on helps you set those much-needed boundaries.

Here's what you can do:

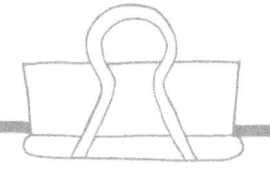

- **Trust Your Gut**: If something feels off, it probably is

- **Observe Their Actions**: Pay attention to whether they display controlling, manipulative, or disrespectful behavior.

- **Self-Reflect**: Think about how their behavior makes you feel—stressed, anxious, or worthless.

Communicating openly with trusted adults or friends about your concerns in a relationship provides insights on setting boundaries. Remember, you're not alone in this. Talking to someone older and wiser can give you a fresh perspective. Sometimes, just explaining what you are going through can help clear your mind and make the path forward more obvious.

Here's a simple guideline to follow:

- **Choose the Right Person**: Talk to someone who has earned your trust, like a parent, teacher, or coach.

- **Be Honest But Tactful**: Explain what's happening without exaggeration.

- **Ask for Their Take**: Sometimes, an outside view can help you see things more clearly.

- **Plan Your Next Steps Together**: Two heads are better than one when planning how to handle a tricky situation.

Establishing clear boundaries through assertive communication is essential. When it comes to maintaining emotional well-being, being assertive is your best weapon. Assertiveness isn't about being aggressive; it's about standing up for yourself in a respectful way. Think of it as planting a "No Trespassing" sign around your emotions and values. Consider this approach:

- **State Your Needs Clearly**: Use "I" statements like, "I feel upset when you talk to me like that."
- **Be Consistent**: Once you set a boundary, stick to it.

- **Practice Makes Perfect**: The more you practice assertive communication, the easier it will become.
- **Stay Calm**: Even if the other person reacts negatively, keep your cool.

Learning to say "No" and prioritizing self-respect is crucial when faced with manipulative behaviors. Saying no can be tough, especially when someone tries to guilt-trip you into doing something you don't want to do. But remember, saying "No" is a form of self-respect—it tells people that you value your own needs and feelings too.

Try these tips:

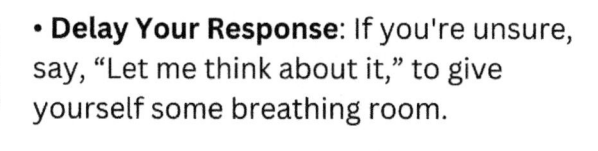

- **Delay Your Response**: If you're unsure, say, "Let me think about it," to give yourself some breathing room.

- **Be Direct but Polite**: A simple, "No, I can't do that," is often enough.

- **Stand Your Ground**: Once you've said no, don't waver unless you really change your mind.

Putting these strategies into practice will significantly improve your ability to maintain healthy relationships. Recognizing toxic patterns early gives you the power to act before things get worse. Communicating your concerns openly builds a support system that can guide you through tough times. Setting boundaries protects your mental and emotional space, allowing you to thrive.

So, next time you encounter a relationship that feels more like a battlefield than a friendship, remember to recognize the signs, speak up, set boundaries, and prioritize your well-being. You've got this!

Respecting Personal Boundaries and Ensuring Mutual Respect

Understanding healthy boundaries and relationships is crucial for teen boys' emotional well-being and growth. Let's dive into what this means and how it can play out in everyday life.

First off, let's talk about understanding and respecting personal space and emotional boundaries of others. Imagine you're in the middle of playing your favorite video game, super focused, and someone just barges into your room without knocking. Annoying, right? That little moment encapsulates why respecting personal space is so important. It fosters trust and respect in relationships. When we respect others' physical and emotional spaces, we're essentially saying, "I see you, I value your comfort."

Now, onto communicating openly about personal boundaries. If you've ever had to deal with a friend who constantly texts or calls at all hours, you know how frustrating it can be.

Here's what you can do to manage those situations:

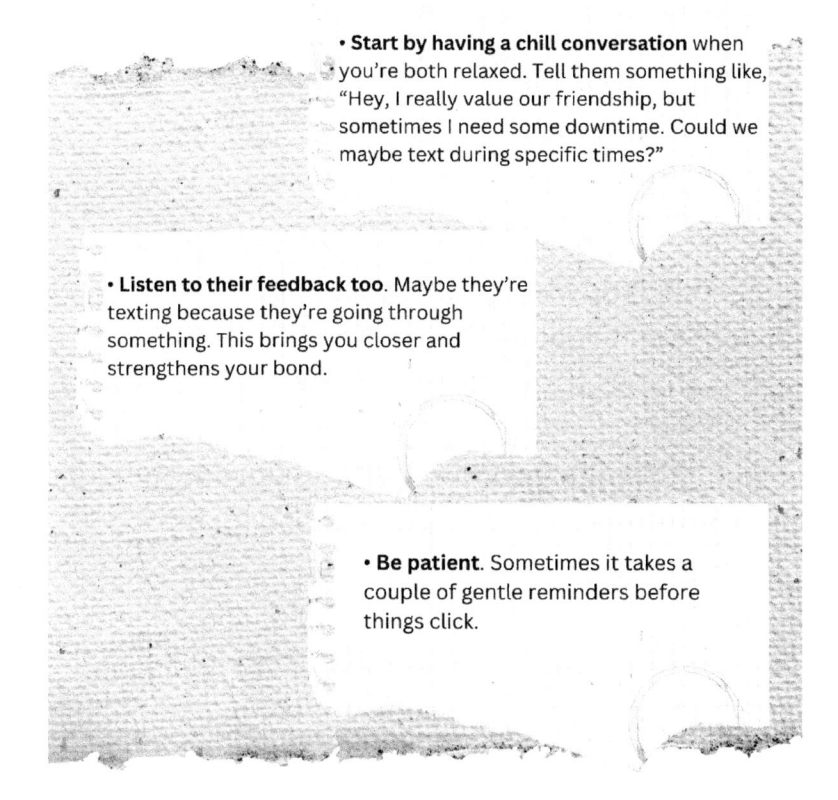

- **Start by having a chill conversation** when you're both relaxed. Tell them something like, "Hey, I really value our friendship, but sometimes I need some downtime. Could we maybe text during specific times?"

- **Listen to their feedback too**. Maybe they're texting because they're going through something. This brings you closer and strengthens your bond.

- **Be patient**. Sometimes it takes a couple of gentle reminders before things click.

Following these steps helps build an environment of mutual respect where everyone feels heard and valued (love is respect, 2023).

Acknowledging and honoring the boundaries set by others demonstrate empathy and care for their well-being. Think about a time when a friend told you something serious and trusted you with that information. Did you listen and respect their feelings? If you did, you showed empathy. Listening to someone when they express a boundary, like not wanting to talk about a stressful topic right now, shows you care about their comfort.

To put this into perspective, imagine your friend says they're uncomfortable joking about certain topics.

Here's a way to handle it:

- **Acknowledge their feelings**: "I didn't realize that bothered you, thanks for letting me know."

- **Change your behavior accordingly**: Actually avoid making those jokes again.

- **Check in occasionally**: "Are we good? Let me know if anything else bothers you."

This demonstrates that you are genuinely considering their feelings and adjusting your behavior to make them feel safe and respected.

Setting boundaries based on personal values and priorities helps maintain a healthy balance in relationships. We all have things that matter to us— whether it's family time, schoolwork, or even alone time for hobbies. Setting boundaries ensures you carve out time for what's important without feeling overwhelmed by other people's demands.

Here's what you can do to set these boundaries effectively:

- **Identify your values:** Take a few moments to think about what truly matters to you. Is it your study time? Your family dinners? Time to just chill and recharge?
- **Communicate clearly:** Share your needs with people around you. "I need to focus on my homework after school, so I might not be able to hang out every day."
- **Be firm yet flexible:** While sticking to your boundaries is important, being understanding if someone needs you will show that you aren't rigidly inflexible.
- **Reevaluate as needed:** Your limits might shift over time. It's okay to revisit and adjust them as you grow and your circumstances change (Institute, 2020).

So, let's recap some notable points: Mutual respect for boundaries and open communication are essential components of maintaining healthy and fulfilling relationships. Knowing how to recognize and honor different types of boundaries can help you build stronger connections and create a supportive environment for yourself and those around you.

Remember, setting and respecting boundaries isn't about putting up walls; it's about creating spaces where everyone feels respected and cared for. By doing so, you're not only enhancing your own well-being but also fostering healthier and more meaningful relationships. And hey, it's totally okay to start small—like asking your friend not to text after midnight unless it's an emergency! Every little step builds towards a more respectful and empathetic world for everyone.

Finally, if you ever feel unsure about navigating any of this, don't hesitate to talk to someone you trust or seek advice from resources available, such as talking to a school counselor or visiting helpful websites (HelpGuide.org, n.d.). It's all about growth, respect, and making sure everyone feels their best.

Effective Ways to Communicate Boundaries and Assert Personal Space

Understanding healthy boundaries is crucial for anyone, and it's super important for teenage boys to get a grip on this early. Healthy boundaries can transform relationships, making them more respectful and enjoyable. But how do you communicate these boundaries and assert personal space without coming off as mean or overly aggressive

First up, let's talk about using "I" statements. Now, you're probably thinking, "What the heck are 'I' statements?" It's pretty straightforward – instead of saying, "You never listen to me!" you say, "I feel unheard when I try to share my thoughts." See the difference? One sparks a fight, while the other opens up a conversation.

Using "I" statements helps convey your needs without making the other person defensive. Imagine this: Your friend Jonas borrows your video game and returns it with a cracked cover. Instead of blaming him outright, you could say, "I felt disappointed when I saw the game's cover was cracked because I take care of my stuff." Your feelings are now out in the open without Jonas feeling attacked.

Here's what you can do to master this:

- Start by identifying your feelings and needs before the conversation.

- Frame your sentences starting with "I feel..." followed by the emotion and the situation.

- Be specific about what behavior affects you and why.

- Avoid blaming or accusing; focus on how you feel.

Next on our list is active listening. This one's a biggie. When discussing boundaries, practicing active listening means really tuning in to what the other person is saying, not just waiting for your turn to speak. Let's say you're telling your friend Austin that you need some alone time to recharge. If Austin starts rolling his eyes or checking his phone, he's clearly not active listening.

To be an active listener:

- **Maintain eye contact and nod** occasionally to show you're engaged.

- **Don't interrupt** – let the other person finish their thoughts.

- **Paraphrase what they've said to show you understand**. Like, "So, you're saying you feel ignored when I don't respond to your texts quickly."

Now, let's talk about setting consequences for boundary violations. Let's face it – no one likes being a pushover. Picture this: You've told your younger brother, Alex, a thousand times not to enter your room without knocking. Yet, here he comes, barging in again. It's time to set some clear, reasonable consequences.

Here's how you can handle it:

- **Restate your boundary clearly.** "Alex, I need privacy in my room. Please knock before entering."
- **Explain the consequence calmly and directly.** "If you come in without knocking again, I'll start locking my door."
- **Follow through with the consequence** if the boundary is violated again.

This approach reinforces the importance of your boundaries and shows that you're serious about maintaining them.

Now, onto asserting personal space and boundaries confidently. This can be tricky, especially if you're dealing with someone who doesn't easily take hints. Imagine you're at a crowded party, and someone's standing way too close. Instead of suffering silently, you can step back and say with a smile, "Hey, I need a little more space."

Assertiveness doesn't mean being rude. It's about being clear and firm.

Here's how to do it:

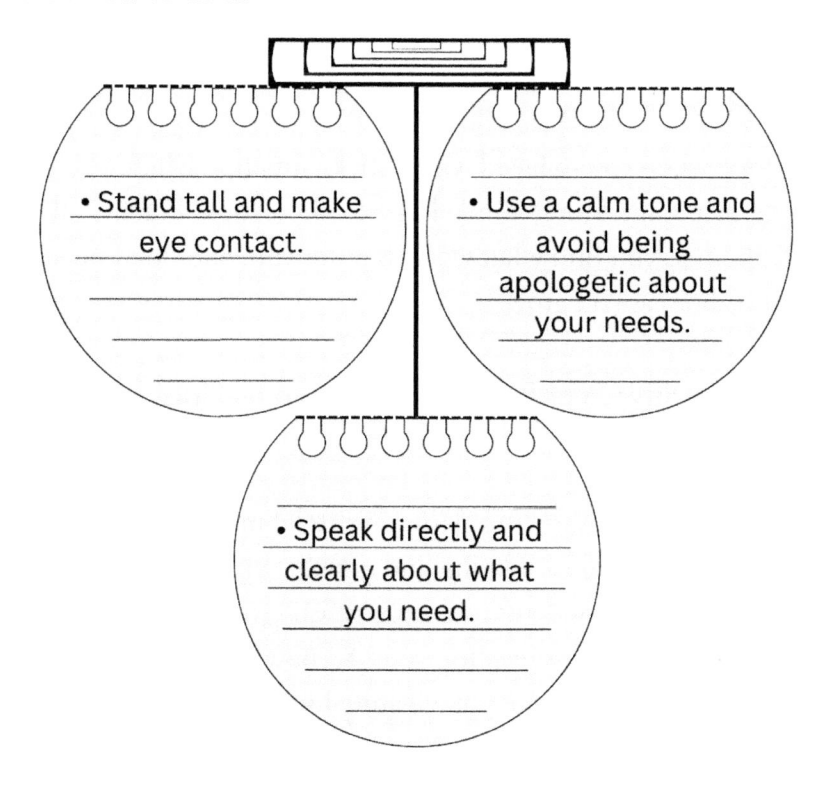

- Stand tall and make eye contact.
- Use a calm tone and avoid being apologetic about your needs.
- Speak directly and clearly about what you need.

Practice makes perfect with all these techniques. The more you use "I" statements, practice active listening, set consequences, and assert your boundaries, the easier it gets. It's like building a muscle – it gets stronger with use.

By understanding and communicating your boundaries effectively, you're setting yourself up for healthier, more rewarding relationships. And hey, having these conversations may seem awkward at first, but they pave the way toward mutual respect and understanding. So give it a go – your future self will thank you!

Remember, boundaries are like invisible fences. They protect your emotional space just as much as physical barriers protect your personal space. And just as important – knowing how to set and maintain those fences will give you the confidence to navigate any relationship smoothly.

Next time when you're faced with a sticky situation where you need to establish some rules, think back to these tips. Practice them, tweak them as you find what works best for you, and don't be afraid to adjust them as you grow.

Building Positive Peer Relationships Based on Trust and Support

Understanding healthy boundaries and relationships is crucial for teen boys' emotional well-being and growth. Building positive peer relationships based on trust and support isn't just nice to have — it's a must-have. It's like assembling your Avengers team, but instead of fighting off evil robots, you're navigating high school and everything life throws at you.

Cultivating Trust Through Honesty and Reliability

Pretend for a minute that you've got a pal named Ben who always shows up when he says he will. Need help with homework? Ben's there. Got tickets to the latest superhero movie? Ben's in the seat next to you. That reliability builds trust. Being honest and reliable makes you someone others can count on, and that's what real friendships are built on. No one wants a flake or a liar as a friend. When you're known for being trustworthy, people naturally gravitate towards you, creating a solid social network. And isn't it cool to know folks have your back?

Offering Support and Empathy

Now, picture your buddy Tim missed out on making the basketball team. Instead of saying, "No big deal," you empathize with him. Maybe you share a time when you were bummed out about something similar and offer to shoot hoops together anyway. Offering support and empathy during tough times fosters bonds built on mutual care. It's not just about being there for the good times—true friends stick around when things get rough. This mutual understanding strengthens your connection, so when you face challenges, you've got a whole squad ready to lift you up.

Respecting Differences and Diverse Perspectives

Think of your friend group as a pizza with different toppings. Some like pepperoni, others prefer veggies, and maybe one loves pineapple. What makes the pizza awesome is the variety. Friendships work the same way. Respecting diverse perspectives means accepting and celebrating differences. Whether it's someone's culture, interests, or opinions, embracing these differences adds flavor to your interactions and promotes tolerance and acceptance. It's okay if you don't agree with everything your friends say or do – that diversity makes your circle richer and teaches everyone to see the world from various angles.

Building Communication Skills to Resolve Conflicts

Conflicts happen; it's part of life. Imagine you and your friend Will disagree on whose turn it is to choose the movie. Instead of letting the situation escalate (cue dramatic background music), use effective communication to resolve it. Here's how:

- **Active Listening:** Start by genuinely listening to Will's point of view without interrupting. Nod, make eye contact, and show you're engaged.

- **Empathy Statements:** Try saying something like, "I get that you feel it should be your turn because we watched my choice last time."

- **Avoid Negative Language:** Instead of saying, "You never let me choose!" go for, "I'd appreciate if we could take turns more fairly."

- **Ask Open-Ended Questions:** Ask Will how he feels the turns could be managed better. This invites a dialogue rather than a confrontation.

- **Summarize Agreements:** Once you've talked it out, summarize what you both agreed on to ensure you're on the same page.

When communicating during conflicts, staying open-minded and non-judgmental helps. Taking breaks if tensions rise and returning to the conversation calmly can prevent escalation. These strategies build a foundation of trust and mutual respect, ensuring conflicts don't damage your friendships but rather strengthen them.

In fact, research supports the significant role of communication in relationships. Effective communication involves exchanging ideas and feelings clearly, focusing on understanding rather than winning an argument, which fosters cooperation and trust (Stiftelsen 29k Foundation, n.d.). So, the way you talk and listen can directly impact how strong your friendships become.

Key Points

1. **Establishing Trust**: Be honest and reliable. Your word is your bond. When people know they can count on you, trust builds naturally.

2. **Providing Support**: Offer empathy and support. Stand by your friends, especially when they're going through tough times. Show them they're not alone.

3. **Fostering Open Communication**: Learn and practice communication skills to resolve conflicts peacefully. Active listening, empathy, and clear, respectful expression of your thoughts can turn potential clashes into opportunities for deeper understanding.

Building positive peer relationships isn't rocket science. It's about being genuine, showing up for each other, and valuing the unique quirks that make each person unique. Think of it like building a championship team – each player has strengths and weaknesses, but together, you're unstoppable. Keep these principles in mind, and you'll not only create lasting friendships but also contribute to a more supportive and understanding community around you.

CHAPTER 9

Coping with Challenges and Adversity

Building Resilience and Adaptability

Imagine yourself skateboarding down your neighborhood street, wind in your hair and the thrill of freedom pumping through your veins. Suddenly, bam! You hit a bump and find yourself sprawled on the pavement, staring up at the sky with scraped knees and bruised pride. What do you do next? Well, you could throw in the towel and vow never to skateboard again. Or, you could dust yourself off, learn what went wrong, and practice until you master that tricky spot. This chapter is all about that second option—building resilience and adaptability so you can face life's bumps, both big and small, head-on.

Consider the hardships you face as various obstacles in your path to success. Some may be simple, such as completing daily tasks or organizing your responsibilities, while others are more challenging— like important examinations, personal conflicts, or familial struggles. Much like navigating through an obstacle course, each life challenge presents an opportunity for personal growth. Yet, it can be unclear how to transform these hurdles into chances for advancement. This is where the importance of cultivating resilience becomes evident. It involves recovering stronger after setbacks, akin to devising a new approach when confronted with a formidable adversary.

In this chapter, you'll dive into developing a growth mindset, transforming failures into stepping stones for success. We'll explore how reflecting on setbacks can fine-tune your approach and make you a better problem-solver. And yes, we will tackle perfectionism

—because nobody expects you to draw a perfect circle freehand on the first try. By the end, you'll have a toolkit of strategies to help you navigate life's ups and downs, turning every stumble into a setup for an epic comeback. Get ready to gear up and face challenges with confidence!

Developing a Growth Mindset

Embracing failures as opportunities for growth can shift perspective and foster resilience. This is a biggie, so let's tackle it head-on. Imagine you're learning to bake a complicated cake for the first time. The first few attempts might result in cakes that are undercooked, overcooked, or just plain messy. Frustrating, right? But here's the thing—every time you bake, you learn something new about the right temperature, the best mixing technique, or the perfect timing. Instead of seeing each imperfect cake as a permanent setback, what if you treat each one as a stepping stone towards finally baking the perfect cake?

> Here's how you can make the most out of every failure:
>
> - **First, recognize that it's okay to fail.** It's part of the process. Think about all those times you've watched blooper reels from your favorite movies. Even the pros mess up!
>
> - **Second, reflect on what went wrong.** Was it a lack of preparation? Maybe you need to dive deeper into your resources.
>
> - **Third, brainstorm different strategies.** If Plan A isn't working, maybe Plan B or C will do the trick.
>
> - **Fourth, try again with these new strategies in mind.** The key is not to give up.

When you start seeing failures as learning experiences, you'll find yourself less stressed and more pumped to take on new challenges (School of Education Online, 2020). It's like turning lemons into lemonade, but way cooler because you're growing stronger and smarter each step of the way.

Understanding that setbacks are part of the learning process builds perseverance and determination. Think about this: Have you ever wondered how many times someone tried to invent a light bulb before it actually worked? Spoiler alert—it was a lot. Thomas Edison supposedly said, "I have not failed. I've just found 10,000 ways that won't work." Setbacks are not roadblocks; they're navigational tools guiding you toward success.

You've got to persist. Look at any sports star or musician—they didn't become great overnight. They faced injuries, rejection, and countless hours of practice. So when life throws you a curveball, see it as a training ground for greatness. Keep pushing forward even when it feels tough, and remember that every hiccup is just another push-up in the gym of life.

Practicing self-reflection after challenges helps identify areas for improvement and personal growth. Let's break this down into bite-sized pieces. After you trip over a hurdle, metaphorical or literal, take a moment to ask yourself, "What did I do there?" "How could I have handled it differently?"

Here's what you can do in order to achieve the goal:

- **Take some time to think about what happened.** Journaling can help you get things organized in your mind.
- **Talk it out with someone you trust.** Sometimes, hearing yourself say things out loud makes solutions pop out of nowhere.
- **Honestly assess your strengths and weaknesses.** It's not about beating yourself up but understanding where you can grow.
- **Make a plan to tackle those weak spots** — maybe through additional practice or seeking advice from someone experienced.

By making self-reflection a habit, you start recognizing patterns in your behavior and thought processes. It's like having a roadmap to better versions of yourself, improving incrementally with each step.

Setting aside perfectionism and embracing mistakes as learning experiences enhances resilience. Oh yes, the dreaded P-word: Perfectionism. It's like trying to draw the perfect circle freehand—it's nearly impossible and often frustrating. Remember, nobody gets everything right on the first try—not even artists, athletes, or engineers. Mistakes are simply part of being human.

Here's how to ditch perfectionism:

- **Accept that you're not perfect, and that's perfectly fine.** Everyone has room to improve.
- **Celebrate your mistakes.** Yes, you read that right. Each mistake is evidence that you're challenging yourself and stepping out of your comfort zone.
- **Replace the word "failure" with "feedback."** When you mess up, see it as valuable information that's going to help you do better next time.
- **Set realistic goals. Aim for progress, not perfection.** Reward yourself for small accomplishments along the way.

By letting go of the need to be perfect, you open yourself up to limitless possibilities. You're not afraid to take risks, which means you're more likely to explore new avenues and discover things you never knew you were capable of doing.

Ultimately, by embracing failures as learning opportunities, understanding setbacks as part of growth, reflecting on challenges for self- improvement, and letting go of perfectionism, you can build resilience and adaptability to face life's ups and downs. These strategies are more than just feel- good mantras; they're backed by tons of research and real-world examples.

Developing a growth mindset isn't just about getting better grades or winning more games; it's about becoming a stronger, more resilient person ready to tackle whatever life throws your way. So, gear up, keep an open mind, and remember, every step—even the backward ones—takes you closer to your goals.

Coping Strategies for Stress and Anxiety

Building resilience and adaptability helps you face challenges and setbacks with determination and strength. It's about equipping you with practical tools you can rely on, especially during the trials of adolescence. Let's dive into some actionable coping strategies that can make a real difference.

First, let's talk about stress-reducing techniques. Life can get overwhelming, whether it's due to exams, social pressures, or just growing pains. Implementing simple practices like deep breathing and mindfulness can be game-changers. Visualize yourself in the middle of a nerve-wracking test; your mind is racing, and every bit of information you crammed seems to vanish. Taking a moment to close your eyes and breathe deeply—inhale for four counts, hold for four, exhale for four, and repeat—can help settle those nerves (Stressors: Coping Skills and Strategies, n.d.).

Here's what you can do to kickstart these techniques:

- ☐ Find a quiet space, even if it's just a bathroom stall.

- ☐ Close your eyes and focus solely on your breath.

- ☐ Inhale slowly through your nose, letting your belly expand.

- ☐ Hold your breath for a few seconds, then exhale through your mouth.

- ☐ Repeat until you feel calmer.

Mindfulness doesn't have to be complicated either. Simply paying attention to the present moment without judgment helps in grounding yourself. Whether it's savoring the taste of a chocolate bar or listening closely to the sounds around you, being mindful means fully engaging with the here and now.

Next up is engaging in physical activities. Regular exercise not only keeps your body fit but also works wonders for your mood. Physical activity releases endorphins—the feel-good hormones—which can ward off feelings of anxiety and depression (Mayo Clinic Health System, n.d.). It doesn't matter whether you're a sports enthusiast or more into solo activities; there's something out there for everyone.

To turn physical activities into a part of your routine:

- Choose something you enjoy, be it skating, cycling, swimming, or even running.

- Set small, achievable goals to avoid feeling overwhelmed.
- Include a friend or two for company, making it a social event rather than a chore.
- Use music or podcasts to make the experience more enjoyable.

Remember, the key is consistency rather than perfection. It's better to go for a 20-minute walk daily than wait until the weekend for a marathon workout session (Anxiety and Depression Association of America, 2024).

Now, let's not overlook the power of social support. Talking about your worries with someone you trust can provide immense relief. The presence of friends, family, or mentors can offer different perspectives that you might not have considered (Stressors: Coping Skills and Strategies, n.d.).

How to seek social support effectively:

- Identify people in your life who are good listeners—friends, family members, teachers, or counselors.
- Don't hesitate to let them know when you need to talk.
- Be honest about what you're going through; often, sharing eases the burden.
- Join clubs or groups where you can meet others with similar interests.

Social interaction isn't just about venting your problems. Sometimes, just hanging out, doing fun activities together, or having a laugh can be incredibly therapeutic. Remember, a balanced life includes both serious conversations and joyous moments.

Prioritizing self-care is equally crucial. Adequate sleep, nutritious eating, and downtime aren't luxuries

—they're essentials. Lack of sleep can exacerbate stress, while poor nutrition can leave you feeling sluggish and irritable. Taking care of your physical health is foundational to overall well-being (Mayo Clinic Health System, n.d.).

Incorporating self-care habits:

- Aim for at least 7-9 hours of sleep each night; a regular sleep schedule helps.
- Eat balanced meals that include plenty of fruits, vegetables, proteins, and whole grains.
- Stay hydrated and limit caffeine and sugar, which can spike anxiety levels.
- Carve out time for activities that relax you, whether it's reading a book, playing video games, or simply chilling out in nature.

You don't have to overhaul your lifestyle overnight. Small, consistent changes lead to significant improvements over time.

Combining these coping strategies sets up a comprehensive approach to handling stress and anxiety. By implementing stress-reducing techniques, engaging in physical activities, seeking social support, and prioritizing self-care, teenage boys can build resilience and adapt to life's inevitable ups and downs. To wrap it up, facing challenges with determination and strength isn't about never stumbling—it's about knowing how to bounce back. It's okay to reach out for help and take proactive steps towards managing stress and anxiety. After all, resilience is built one step at a time, and every effort counts.

Seeking Support During Adversity

When life throws you a curveball, having someone to talk to can make all the difference. So, let's dive in and talk about why reaching out for support is a game-changer and how it can help you tackle challenges head-on.

First off, talking openly with trusted individuals— think friends, family, or even that cool teacher who gets you—can offer you new ways to see a problem and emotional encouragement at the same time. It's like having your own squad of coaches when you're down 20 points in the fourth quarter. They give you different plays and cheer you on.

Here's what you can do to maximize this:

- **Identify your go-to people**: These could be anyone you trust and feel comfortable opening up to.

- **Set the stage**: Find a quiet moment and place to have these conversations without distractions.

- **Be honest**: Lay your problems out there. Sometimes, just saying things out loud helps you understand them better.

- **Listen to feedback**: Your friends and family might see solutions you haven't thought of.

Research backs this up! The Urban Child Institute highlights how social support can buffer against stress and improve overall well-being (Social Support Can Help Break the Cycle of Adversity, n.d.).

Now, we've all seen those movie scenes where the hero finally decides to seek professional help, and it's always a dramatic turning point. Recognizing signs that you might need some expert intervention isn't as flashy but super important. You might be dealing with stuff that's just too much to handle alone, and knowing when to reach out for professional help can seriously save the day. **Here are some tips to figure out if it's time to call in the pros:**

- **Notice persistent feelings**: If sadness, anxiety, or anger stick around for weeks and mess with your daily life, it's time to consider talking to someone.

- **Check your reactions**: Are you reacting way more strongly to situations than usual? Like flipping out over small stuff?

- **Physical symptoms**: Stuff like headaches, stomachaches, or trouble sleeping can sometimes be tied to emotional stress.

- **Talk to someone you trust**: They might notice changes in you that you haven't seen yourself.

Reaching out isn't admitting defeat; it's gearing up for battle with the right tools. Plus, professionals offer coping strategies tailored to help you navigate your unique set of challenges. According to Greater Good, social support in its many forms is crucial in resilience-building (Greater Good, n.d.).

Next up, let's talk about building that strong support network of friends and family. Think of it like constructing your personal fortress. When you have a bunch of supportive relationships, you create a sense of belonging and security that keeps you grounded during rough patches. Your buddies and family are like the bricks and mortar that keep you standing tall.

So, how do you go about strengthening these connections?

- **Show genuine interest:** Ask how they're doing and really listen.
- **Spend quality time together:** Whether it's playing video games, grabbing burgers, or just hanging out, these moments build bonds.
- **Be there for them too:** Support is a two-way street. Make sure you're also a shoulder to lean on when they need it.
- **Communicate regularly:** Keep in touch! A quick text or a funny meme can keep the connection alive.

It's scientifically proven that good social relationships matter. A study highlighted by Social Support and Resilience to Stress showcases how positive social ties can enhance psychological and physical health (Charney et al., n.d.).

Finally, let's debunk the idea that asking for help is a sign of weakness. Actually, it's quite the opposite. Understanding that seeking help demonstrates strength promotes mental well-being. It shows that you recognize your limits and are proactive about solving issues. It's similar to an athlete hiring a coach to improve their performance—not because they're bad, but because they want to be better. Embrace reaching out for help as a positive step forward:

- **Normalize it:** Talk openly about needing help. Everyone has times when they need a hand.
- **Share your experiences:** When you open up about your struggles, you might find others feel the same way and are inspired to seek help themselves.

- **View it as growth:** Understand that every time you ask for help, you're learning and growing, both mentally and emotionally.

Let's face it, everyone needs a little backup now and then. Even superheroes have sidekicks.

In conclusion, remember the key takeaways here: communicate openly with trusted individuals, recognize when professional help may be needed, build a strong support network, and embrace seeking help as a sign of strength. Life's challenges may be tough, but with the right support and strategies, you can build resilience and adaptability to face whatever comes your way. And hey, don't forget to laugh along the journey—it makes the bumps easier to bear.

Turning Challenges into Opportunities

Dealing with challenges and setbacks is part of growing up, but it's how you face them that really defines your character. So, let's talk about turning those roadblocks into stepping stones for personal growth and development.

First up, let's chat about viewing challenges as opportunities for learning. Imagine facing a daunting math test or getting benched in your favorite sport. It's easy to feel defeated, but what if you flipped the script? See each challenge as a chance to learn something new. For example, that tough math problem? It's an opportunity to sharpen your problem-solving skills. Getting benched? Time to up your practice game and analyze what can make you better. When you embrace this mindset, you're not just tackling the issue at hand, but also building invaluable skills for the future.

Here's what you can do:

> **Here's what you can do:**
>
> • Start by identifying the specific challenge you're facing.
>
> • Break it down into smaller parts and figure out what skills you need to tackle each part.
>
> • Seek out resources—books, online tutorials, or even asking a teacher or coach for help.
>
> • Apply what you've learned and reflect on the outcome, making adjustments as needed.

Next, setting realistic goals to overcome challenges gradually can work wonders for building confidence and resilience. Say you're struggling with running the mile in gym class. Instead of aiming to break a record right off the bat, set smaller, achievable targets. Maybe start by improving your time by a few seconds each week. This approach boosts your confidence as you meet each mini-goal and makes the overall objective seem less intimidating.

To get started:

- Define your end goal clearly.
- Break this goal into smaller, manageable steps or milestones.
- Track your progress regularly to stay motivated.
- Celebrate small victories along the way to keep your spirits high.

Now, let's dive into embracing change and adaptation during challenges. Change is inevitable, whether it's moving to a new school, adjusting to a new family dynamic, or even dealing with unexpected events like a pandemic. The key is to be flexible and adaptable.

Think of it like riding a wave: instead of fighting against it, learn to move with it. Embracing change helps you develop a more resilient and flexible mindset, preparing you for the twists and turns life throws your way. As one intern beautifully put it while working at Chilcotin Holidays ranch, circumstances changing is inevitable, but growth isn't. You have to consciously take on new things with an open mind and a positive attitude if you want to grow (horsie, 2020).

Here's a structured way to adapt:

- Accept that change is a natural part of life.

- Stay curious and open-minded; ask questions and seek understanding.

- Focus on what you can control and let go of what you can't.

- Develop a routine that includes time for reflection and self-care to maintain mental well-being.

Last but definitely not least, reflecting on past adversities and how you've overcome them can provide motivation and strength for future challenges. Think back to a time when you faced something tough. How did you get through it? What strategies worked for you? Reflecting on these experiences not only reminds you of your resilience but also equips you with a toolkit for future challenges. This reflection can boost your confidence and remind you that you've got what it takes to handle whatever comes your way.

Reflecting can be done effectively by:

- Keeping a journal where you jot down significant challenges and how you overcame them.

- Regularly reviewing your entries to track your progress and identify patterns.

- Discussing your reflections with a trusted mentor, friend, or family member to gain additional perspectives.

So, let's wrap all these teachings into main ideas. When you see challenges as learning opportunities, set achievable goals for growth, embrace change during hardships, and draw strength from overcoming past adversities, you're essentially building a powerhouse of resilience and adaptability. These traits are not just handy for surviving the teenage years but are crucial life skills that will serve you in adulthood too.

Developing resilience and adaptability is not about having a superhero-like ability to bounce back from everything unscathed; it's about facing challenges head-on, learning from the experience, and emerging stronger. By incorporating the steps and guidelines mentioned, you'll find that what once seemed like insurmountable obstacles are now valuable lessons disguised as challenges.

Remember, every setback is a setup for a comeback. Keep pushing, stay curious, and most importantly, believe in yourself. With every challenge you conquer, you're not just getting through it—you're growing through it.

CHAPTER 10

Planning for the Future- Career and Education

Setting Long-Term Goals and Planning for the Future

Picture yourself standing at the edge of a vast, uncharted forest, armed only with a compass and a slightly crumpled treasure map. It's as exciting as it is daunting, right? Setting long-term goals and planning for the future can feel a lot like embarking on an epic quest. For you, this journey isn't just about picking which college to apply to or deciding on a career—it's about charting a path through life that's uniquely yours. It's your adventure, and this chapter is here to ensure you're well-prepared to navigate it.

Now, let's dive into why setting these goals is a game- changer. Imagine waking up each day without a sense of direction—like playing a video game but having no clue what the objective is. You'd wander aimlessly, completing random tasks with no clear purpose. It's the same in real life. Without long-term goals, it's easy to get lost in the shuffle of school assignments, part-time jobs, and weekend plans. For instance, maybe you're passionate about video game design, but instead of actively seeking out coding classes or internships, you spend all your time playing games. Fun, sure, but not exactly productive. Or perhaps you dream of being an environmental scientist, yet you've never looked into the necessary education or started networking with professionals in the field.

That's where setting goals comes into play—it gives you a roadmap so you can focus on what truly matters.

In this chapter, we'll break down the art of setting long-term goals and planning for the future into manageable steps that even the busiest of teens can tackle. We'll explore how to identify your passions and interests through various career assessment tools and research methods. You'll learn the ins and outs of shadowing professionals and securing internships to gain firsthand experience. We'll also delve into effective ways to network and build relationships with mentors who can guide you along the way. By the end, you'll have a solid plan to help you navigate your academic and career paths with confidence and clarity. So grab that metaphorical compass and treasure map—your adventure awaits!

Exploring Career Paths and Interests

Exploring different career paths and interests to make informed decisions is like planning a road trip. You wouldn't just hop in the car and start driving without a map or a destination in mind, right? It's essential for you to set long-term goals and plan for your future now, so you can navigate through the world of education and careers with confidence and clarity.

First up, let's talk about researching various career fields and industries. This might sound boring, but think of it as detective work. Digging into different jobs can reveal surprising opportunities that you'd never considered before. From architecture to being a doctor, the options are endless. Use online resources and career exploration websites to get started. The O*NET® Career Exploration Tools are a gold mine for this (*O NET® Career

Exploration Tools at O *NET Resource Center*). They offer an Interest Profiler that helps match your interests with potential careers. Plus, they describe over 900 occupations, making it easy to picture what each job entails.

Now, let's get to something more hands-on: shadowing professionals or participating in internships. This isn't just about sitting in an office all day; it's about experiencing a day in the life of someone working in your field of interest.

Here's what you can do to get the most out of this experience:

- Start by reaching out to professionals in careers you're curious about. A simple email or phone call can open doors.

- When you get the chance to shadow someone, pay attention to everything – from their main tasks to how they interact with colleagues.

- Ask questions. Lots of them. You're there to learn, so don't hold back.

- Reflect on the experience afterward. Did you enjoy it? What aspects intrigued you? This can help refine your career choices.

Internships are another excellent way to gain practical experience. Many companies offer summer programs specifically for high school students. These don't just look good on college applications; they give you a genuine taste of what working in a particular industry feels like.

Utilizing career assessment tools can also be incredibly beneficial. It's Your Yale offers several types of assessments focusing on interests, personality, and skills (Yale University. (n.d.). *Career assessment tools*).

Here's a quick guide on how to use these tools effectively:

- **Start with an interest-based assessment** like the O*NET Interest Profiler. This will help identify what kinds of activities you enjoy.
- **Next, take a personality test.** Understanding your personality can help match you with work environments where you'll thrive.
- **Finally, assess your skills.** Tools like the DiSC Behavior Inventory or CareerOneStop Skills Center can highlight your strengths and areas for development.

Combining the results from these different assessments gives you a fuller picture of careers where you're likely to be both successful and happy.

Another powerful way to explore different career paths is networking with professionals. Now, I know this sounds a bit grown-up and intimidating, but it's just about talking and building connections.

Here's how you can go about it:

> - **Start with people you know.** Parents, teachers, friends' parents – ask them about their careers and any advice they might have for you.
>
> - **Attend career fairs and workshops.** These events are great for meeting professionals and learning about various industries.
>
> - **Use social media wisely.** Platforms like LinkedIn can connect you with professionals and organizations in fields that interest you.
>
> - **Don't be shy to request informational interviews.** This is just a fancy term for chatting with someone about their job and career path. Prepare a few questions beforehand to make the most of their time.

All these steps can help you gather valuable insights and advice, making your career exploration journey more comprehensive and informed. By exploring diverse career options and seeking guidance, you not only broaden your horizons but also empower yourself to make well-informed decisions. Remember, setting long-term goals and planning for your future doesn't mean locking yourself into one path forever. It's about giving yourself direction and purpose, knowing that adjustments along the way are part of the process.

So, let's sum it all up. To set yourself up for success:

- **Dive deep into researching various careers.** Use tools like the O*NET® Career Exploration Tools (Author Last Name, Year) to understand the opportunities that align with your interests.

- **Get out there and gain practical experience through shadowing and internships.** Every moment spent in a real-world job environment can be enlightening.

- **Harness the power of career assessment tools** to match your interests, personality, and skills with suitable career paths.
- **Build a network of professionals who can provide insights and advice.** Their experiences and knowledge can be invaluable in shaping your career decisions.

Success in your career and education begins with the steps you take today. The path may be winding and sometimes uncertain, but with thorough exploration and thoughtful planning, you'll find your way. So, grab that map, chart your course, and embark on this exciting journey towards your future.

Preparing for College or Vocational Training

When it comes to planning for the future, setting long-term goals and preparing for college or vocational training is essential for you. It's like training for a major sports tournament—you need strategy, consistent practice, and a clear vision of the championship to succeed. In this section, we're going to walk you through some practical tips and advice on how to get ready for your next big adventure.

Let's kick things off with researching different educational paths. Think of this as your scouting mission. Colleges, universities, and vocational programs each have their unique perks and challenges. The goal here isn't just about picking a school—it's about finding the right fit for you and your ambitions. Are you more into hands-on learning, or do you thrive in a traditional classroom setting? Understanding these preferences can help you narrow down your choices. You wouldn't jump into a game without checking out the reviews, right? Treat your education the same way by visiting campuses, talking to current students, and comparing curricula. Next up, understanding admission requirements and deadlines for your desired institutions. This is your quest log—a must-have to keep track of what you need to do and when.

Here's what you can do:

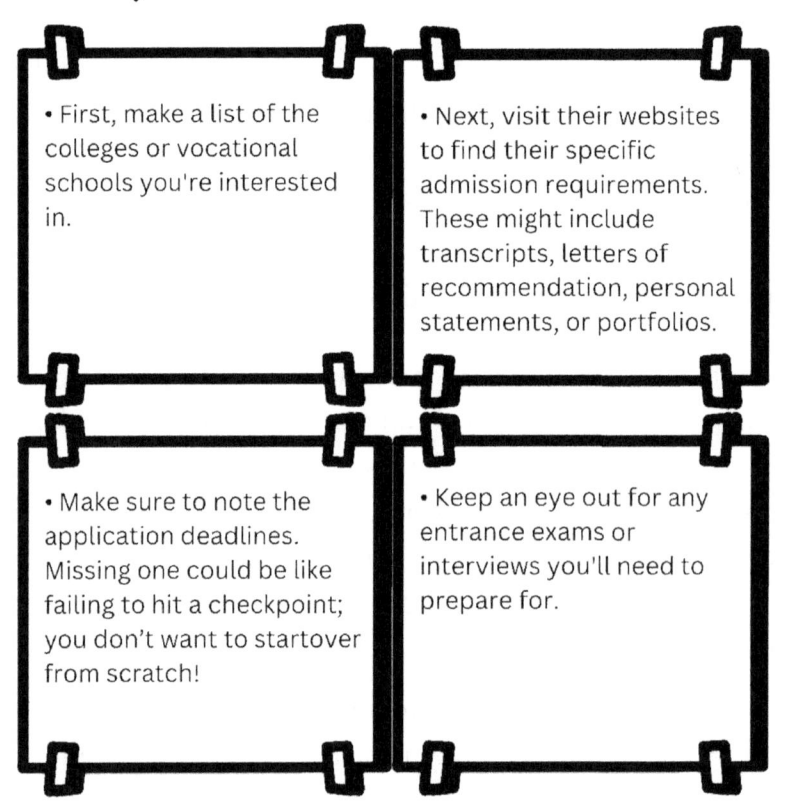

- First, make a list of the colleges or vocational schools you're interested in.

- Next, visit their websites to find their specific admission requirements. These might include transcripts, letters of recommendation, personal statements, or portfolios.

- Make sure to note the application deadlines. Missing one could be like failing to hit a checkpoint; you don't want to startover from scratch!

- Keep an eye out for any entrance exams or interviews you'll need to prepare for.

Creating a study plan and prepping for standardized tests like the SAT or ACT are similar to preparing for a big performance. You'll need discipline, consistent practice, and a well-thought-out strategy.

Here's what you can do to ace this:

- Start by assessing your current strengths and weaknesses. Take a few practice tests to see where you stand.

- Set a realistic timeline for studying and stick to it. Break down your study sessions into manageable chunks rather than cramming all at once.

- Use a variety of study materials, such as prep books, online courses, and flashcards. Mix it up to keep yourself engaged.

- Don't forget to include breaks and rewards. After all, even the best gamers need downtime to relax and recharge.

Navigating the world of scholarships, grants, and financial aid can feel like unlocking hidden treasure in a game. It's crucial to support your educational goals without getting buried under a mountain of student debt.

Follow these steps to secure your loot:

- **Research various scholarship opportunities early on.** Many have specific criteria, such as academic performance, extracurricular involvement, or essay submissions.

- **Fill out the Free Application for Federal Student Aid (FAFSA) to see what federal aid you qualify for.** Deadlines vary by state, so mark your calendar.

- **Look into grants and work-study programs offered by your chosen institutions.** These can significantly reduce your financial burden while providing valuable work experience.
- **Don't hesitate to apply for multiple scholarships and grants.** Each one increases your chances of getting the financial support you need.

Early planning and preparation are your secret weapons in this journey. Whether you opt for college or vocational training, starting early gives you the time to explore options, meet requirements, and gather resources without feeling rushed or overwhelmed.

Remember, you're not alone in this quest. Seek guidance from your family, teachers, and career counselors. They can offer valuable insights and support every step of the way.

Your future is a choose-your-adventure story, and with careful planning and perseverance, you'll write a chapter that leads to success.

By breaking down these steps and approaching them methodically, you can ensure you're well-prepared for whatever educational path you choose. Embrace the challenge with an open mind and a determined spirit

—it's the same mindset that great adventurers and successful individuals have used to overcome obstacles and achieve their dreams.

Prepare yourself, stay focused, and may your future endeavors be as exciting and fulfilling as your wildest dreams. Embrace each challenge with determination and enthusiasm, and remember that every step you take brings you closer to your goals.

Setting Academic Goals and Developing a Study Plan

Setting academic goals and developing a study plan for success

Establish SMART Goals

Picture this: You, just aced that tough math test, and there's a big grin plastered across your face. How did you get here? By setting SMART goals! Now, I'm not talking about the regular "get good grades" kind of goal. Nah, we're going deeper. SMART stands for Specific, Measurable, Achievable, Relevant, and Time-bound.

Here's the deal with SMART goals:

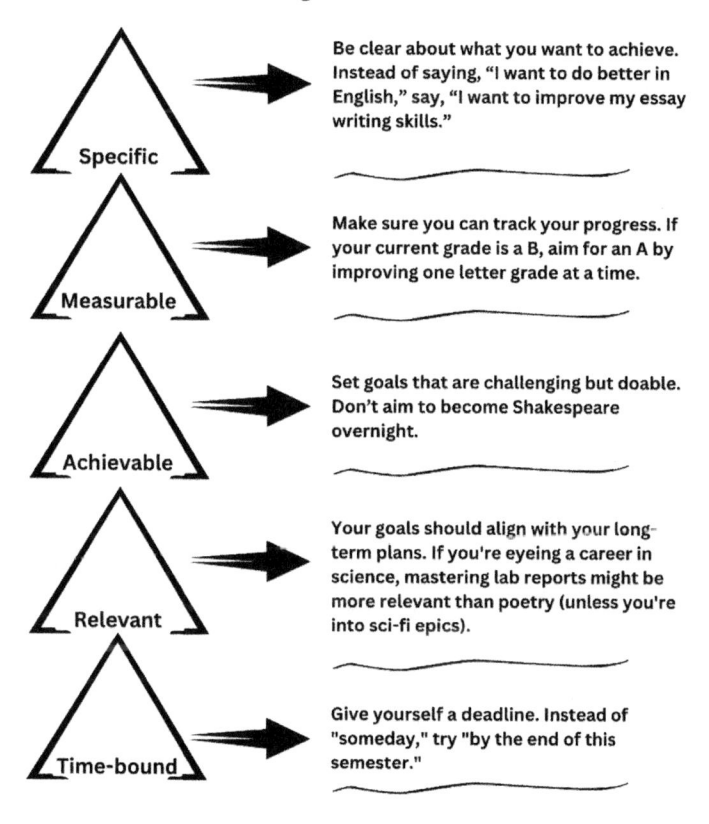

Specific → Be clear about what you want to achieve. Instead of saying, "I want to do better in English," say, "I want to improve my essay writing skills."

Measurable → Make sure you can track your progress. If your current grade is a B, aim for an A by improving one letter grade at a time.

Achievable → Set goals that are challenging but doable. Don't aim to become Shakespeare overnight.

Relevant → Your goals should align with your long-term plans. If you're eyeing a career in science, mastering lab reports might be more relevant than poetry (unless you're into sci-fi epics).

Time-bound → Give yourself a deadline. Instead of "someday," try "by the end of this semester."

When you make your goals SMART, they go from vague dreams to tangible targets. It's like turning on the GPS for your academic journey.

Create a Study Schedule

Alright, so you've got your goals. The next step is to craft a killer study schedule. Think of it as a game plan, like those strategy maps in video games. You wouldn't rush headfirst into a boss battle without a plan, right?

Here are some quick tips for creating an effective study schedule:

- **Allocate time wisely**: Balance your homework, test prep, and some self-study. Don't forget to squeeze in moments for breaks – nobody likes brain burnout.

- **Consistency rules:** Try to study at the same time each day. Making it a habit helps your brain know it's game time.

- **Mix it up**: Rotate subjects to keep things fresh and exciting. Math today, history tomorrow, and maybe some science after that.

Having a visual guide, whether it's a digital calendar or a good old-fashioned planner, can help keep you on track. Plus, crossing off completed tasks feels pretty awesome, trust me.

Seek Academic Support

Even superheroes need sidekicks, right? So don't hesitate to seek academic support when tackling those villainous algebra problems or pesky essay prompts. Whether it's tutoring, study groups, or mentorship programs, getting help is a wise move.

Here's what you can do:

- **Tutoring**: Find someone who gets the stuff you don't. Sometimes, a different explanation can make all the difference.

- **Study groups**: Team up with classmates. Learning together can spark new ideas and make studying less dull.

- **Mentorship**: Look for a mentor who has been there, done that. They can offer valuable advice and guidance.

By seeking support, you're not just learning the material; you're also figuring out how to ask for help when you need it. That's a life skill that pays off in more ways than one.

Monitor Progress Regularly

You've set goals, built a schedule, and sought support. Now comes the part where you monitor your progress like a scientist tracking an experiment.

Here's how to keep your academic engine running smoothly:

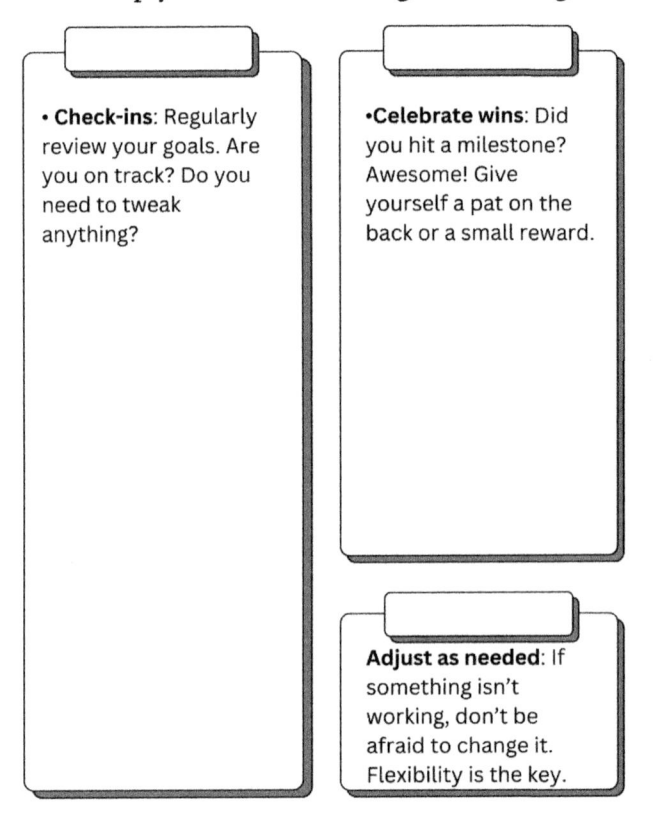

- **Check-ins**: Regularly review your goals. Are you on track? Do you need to tweak anything?

- **Celebrate wins**: Did you hit a milestone? Awesome! Give yourself a pat on the back or a small reward.

- **Adjust as needed**: If something isn't working, don't be afraid to change it. Flexibility is the key.

Think of this stage as fine-tuning a musical instrument. It's about making small adjustments that can lead to significant improvements over time, just like perfecting your technique to produce the best sound.

Alright, let's wrap this up with some key takeaways. Prioritizing academic success through goal-setting and effective study habits isn't just about earning high grades — it's about developing skills that will serve you throughout life.

Here's what you should remember:

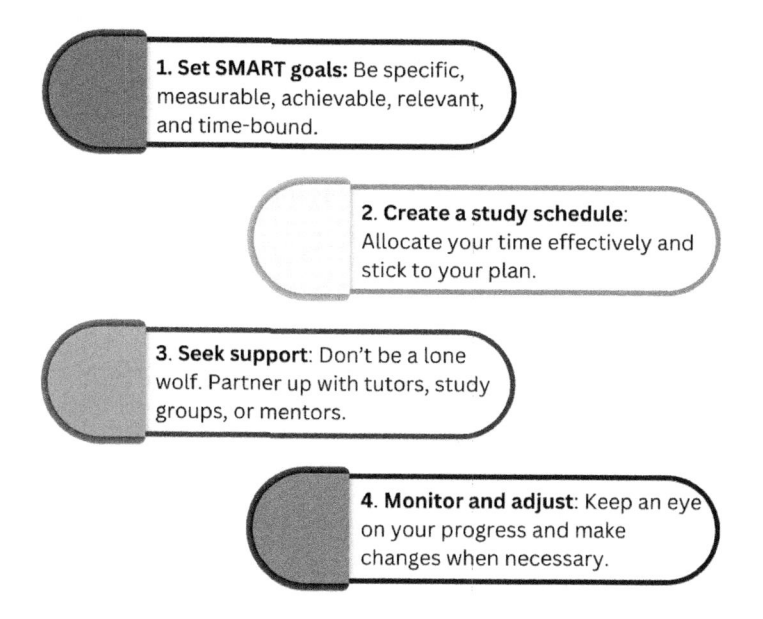

1. **Set SMART goals:** Be specific, measurable, achievable, relevant, and time-bound.

2. **Create a study schedule:** Allocate your time effectively and stick to your plan.

3. **Seek support:** Don't be a lone wolf. Partner up with tutors, study groups, or mentors.

4. **Monitor and adjust:** Keep an eye on your progress and make changes when necessary.

Remember, the path to success is not a straight line. There will be twists and turns, ups and downs. But with the right goals and strategies in place, you'll be well-equipped to navigate the journey. And who knows? You might even enjoy the ride. Keep pushing forward, stay curious, and most importantly, believe in your ability to achieve greatness.

Developing Networking Skills and Building Professional Relationships

Expanding your professional connections is like leveling up in a game; it's all about strategy, timing, and sometimes a bit of courage. Here's the lowdown on how to do it right. First off, attending career fairs, networking events, and setting up informational interviews are golden opportunities to turbocharge your network. Imagine these events as treasure hunts, but instead of gold coins or rare artifacts, you're collecting valuable relationships that can shape your future. What's great about these events is that everyone's there for the same reason—to meet, connect, and explore potential opportunities. So don't be shy!

Here's how you can make the most out of them:

- **Preparation is Key**: Before heading to any event, do some homework. Research who will be attending, understand their roles, and think about how they might fit into your career puzzle.
- **Craft Your Elevator Pitch**: Have a quick introduction ready. In the time it takes an elevator to go from floor to floor, you should be able to tell someone who you are, what you do, and what you're hoping to achieve.
- **Engage Genuinely**: Don't just collect business cards like Pokémon. Try to have meaningful conversations. Ask open-ended questions to really get to know the person.
- **Follow Up**: After the event, send a quick email or LinkedIn message to thank them for their time and mention something specific you discussed to jog their memory.

Building a professional online presence is another crucial step. Think of your LinkedIn profile as your digital business card—one that doesn't get lost in someone's wallet.

To maximize your online presence:

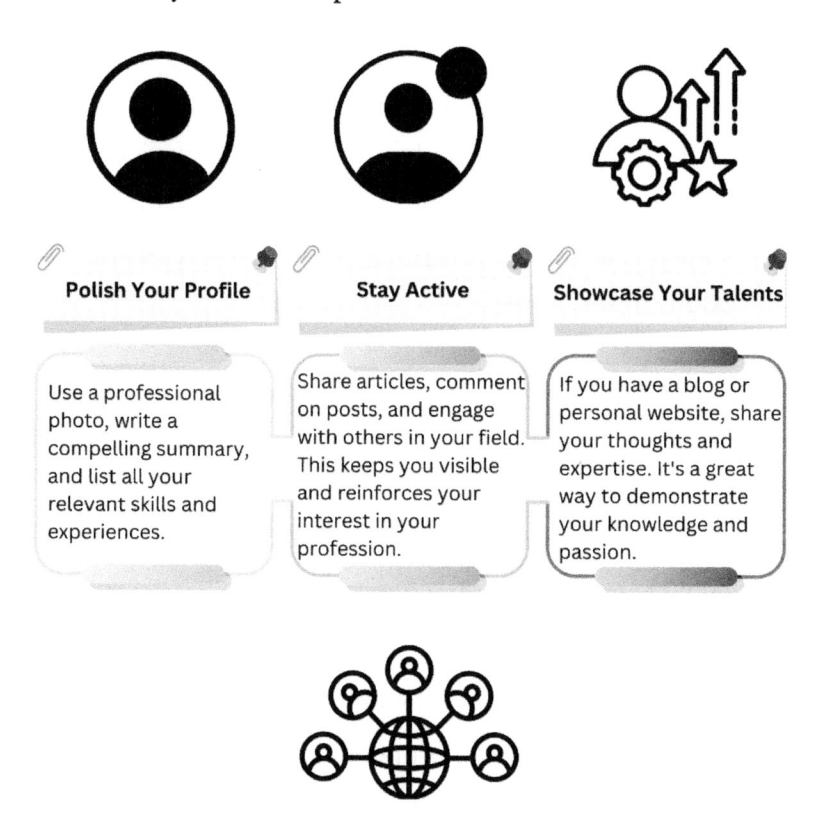

Polish Your Profile

Use a professional photo, write a compelling summary, and list all your relevant skills and experiences.

Stay Active

Share articles, comment on posts, and engage with others in your field. This keeps you visible and reinforces your interest in your profession.

Showcase Your Talents

If you have a blog or personal website, share your thoughts and expertise. It's a great way to demonstrate your knowledge and passion.

Volunteering or engaging in extracurricular activities is where you build those soft skills that aren't always taught in school but are invaluable in the professional world. Leadership and communication skills can't be overemphasized. Whether it's leading a team for a community project or organizing a club at school, these experiences teach you how to work with others, manage conflicts, and motivate people.

To really benefit from volunteering:

- **Choose Wisely**: Pick activities that align with your interests or intended career path. Passion projects often bring out the best in us.

- **Take Initiative**: Don't wait for opportunities to fall into your lap. Volunteer for leadership roles or start a project yourself.

- **Reflect and Learn**: After each experience, take some time to reflect on what you learned and how you can apply these lessons in the future.

Maintaining contact with mentors, teachers, and professionals in your desired career fields is like having a map while navigating uncharted territory. These individuals have been through the thick of it and can provide invaluable advice and support.

Here's how to keep those connections strong:

- **Regular Check-ins**: Drop a line every now and then to share updates about your progress and ask for advice.

- **Show Appreciation**: A simple thank-you note can go a long way in maintaining goodwill.

- **Seek Feedback**: Don't hesitate to ask for constructive criticism. It shows that you're serious about growth and value their opinion.

The importance of networking and relationship- building for future career growth cannot be overstated. Research suggests that successful leaders excel because they master different forms of networking (Harvard Business Review, 2007). Networking isn't just about adding contacts to your phonebook; it's about creating a web of meaningful relationships that provide support, feedback, and resources throughout your career.

A robust network helps you discover new job openings, provides referrals, and offers guidance during challenging times (Marquette, 2023). It's a dynamic, living system that evolves with you, offering continuous opportunities for learning and advancement.

So, why wait? Start building your network today. Attend events, polish that LinkedIn profile, volunteer, and keep in touch with your mentors. Remember, it's not just about what you know, but who you know— and who knows you. And hey, don't forget to have fun along the way! Networking isn't just a chore; it can be a rewarding part of your career journey, bringing you closer to your goals one connection at a time.

Looking Forward with Confidence

Alright, let's bring this to an exciting close! We've covered some awesome skills that can make your everyday life feel like an epic adventure. Emotional intelligence, confidence, effective communication, time management, health, resilience, and relationships—these are all the superpowers you need to navigate the rocky road of teenagehood.

You've got a toolbox packed with critical life skills. By tuning into your emotions, firing up your confidence, and mastering the art of talking and listening, you're gearing up for success. Think of it as training for a big competition—every small step counts toward achieving your ultimate goal.

But here's the kicker: knowing these skills isn't enough. You've gotta put them into practice. Imagine facing each day not just with the aim of surviving but thriving. That means embracing those awkward moments, nailing your school projects, and even dealing with that part-time job with more finesse than ever before. You have all these tools at your disposal—it's like having an all-access pass to a behind-the-scenes tour of adulting.

Now, it's normal to worry a bit. Will you mess up? Probably. Will things always go according to plan? Definitely not. But that's where resilience comes in. It's like getting a fresh start in a new race—no matter how many times you stumble, you get to try again. The key is to keep learning and growing from every little experience. On a bigger scale, imagine if every teen boy started applying these lessons. We'd have a generation of thoughtful, confident, and resilient individuals ready to tackle whatever life throws at them. These aren't just skills; they're building blocks for a well-rounded, fulfilling life.

So, look at today as your starting line. Whether you're staring down the barrel of a tough exam or figuring out how to talk to someone new, remember you've got what it takes. Apply these lessons, make them yours, and watch yourself transform. Who knows? Maybe one day, someone will tell your story to inspire others, just like Caleb's.

You've got this, my friend. Now go out there and show life who's the boss!

References

Introduction

Hellström, L., & Beckman, L. (2021). *Life challenges and barriers to help seeking: Adolescents' and young adults' voices of mental health.* International Journal of Environmental Research and Public Health, 18(24), 13101. https://doi.org/10.3390/ijerph182413101

Campbell-Heider, N., Tuttle, J., & Knapp, T. R. (2009). *The effect of positive adolescent life skills training on long-term outcomes for high-risk teens.* Journal of Addictions Nursing, 20(6), 1-10. https://doi.org/10.1080/10884600802693165

UNICEF. (n.d.). *Around 3 in 4 youth lack skills needed for employment, new report says.* UNICEF. https://www.unicef.org/press-releases/around-3-4-youth-lack-skills-needed-employment-new-report-says

Anderson, A. (2023). *Lost life skills – Our youth are not being taught necessary life skills. JumpIn Northwest.* Retrieved from https://www.jump-in.org/blog/2023/12/12/lost-life-skills-our-youth-are-not-being-taught-necessary-life-skills

Chapter 1

Feder, M. (2023). *Understanding imposter syndrome in college students. University of Phoenix*

Retrieved from https://www.phoenix.edu/blog/impostor-syndrome.html

Action For Happiness. (n.d.). *Set your goals and make them happen*. Retrieved from https://actionforhappiness.org/take-action/set-your-goals-and-make-them-happen

HelpGuide. (n.d.). *Effective Communication: Improving Your Interpersonal Skills*. Retrieved from https://www.helpguide.org/articles/relationships-communication/effective-communication.htm

Skylight. (n.d.). *Affirmations for self-esteem and why they work*. Retrieved from https://skylight.org/blog/posts/affirmations-for-self-esteem-and-why-they-work

Harvard Extension School. (2024). How to Create an *Action Plan to Achieve Your Goals*. Retrieved from https://extension.harvard.edu/blog/how-to-create-an-action-plan-to-achieve-your-goals/

Cleveland Clinic. (n.d.). *What's Imposter Syndrome and How To Overcome It*. Cleveland Clinic. Retrieved from https://health.clevelandclinic.org/a-psychologist-explains-how-to-deal-with-imposter-syndrome

Mayo Clinic. (2024). *Being assertive: Reduce stress, communicate better. Mayo Clinic*. Retrieved from https://www.mayoclinic.org/healthy-lifestyle/stress-management/in-depth/assertive/art-20044644

Colorado University. (2024). *Must-try tips for setting (and accomplishing) your goals this year. Health & Wellness Services*. Retrieved from https://www.colorado.edu/health/blog/goal-setting

Simply Psychology. (2023). *Learn Assertive Communication in 5 Simple Steps. Simply Psychology.* Retrieved from https://www.simplypsychology.org/assertive-communication.html.

Chapter 2

Utah State University. (n.d.). *Body Image in Adolescence.* Retrieved from https://extension.usu.edu/nutrition/research/body-image-in-adolescence

MyPlate. (n.d.). *Life stages: Teens.* Retrieved from https://www.myplate.gov/life-stages/teens

National Institute of Diabetes and Digestive and Kidney Diseases. (2024). *Take Charge of Your Health: A Guide for Teenagers.* Retrieved from https://www.niddk.nih.gov/health-information/weight-management/take-charge-health-guide-teenagers

Guo, Z., & Zhang, Y. (2022). *Study on the Interactive Factors between Physical Exercise and Mental Health Promotion of Teenagers. Journal of Healthcare Engineering.* https://doi.org/10.1155/2022/4750133

University of Rochester Medical Center. *Hypercalcemia.* Retrieved from https://www.urmc.rochester.edu/encyclopedia/content.aspx?ContentTypeID=90&ContentID=P01602

AACAP. (n.d.). *Helping teenagers with stress.* https://www.aacap.org/AACAP/Families_and_Youth/Facts_for_Families/FFF-Guide/Helping-Teenagers-With-Stress-066.aspx

Tort-Nasarre, G., Pollina-Pocallet, M., Ferrer Suquet, Y., Ortega Bravo, M., Vilafranca Cartagena, M., & Artigues-Barberà, E. (2023). *Positive body image: a qualitative study on the successful experiences of adolescents, teachers and parents. International Journal of Qualitative Studies on Health and Well- being,* 18(1), 10.1080/17482631.2023.2170007.

https://doi.org/10.1080/17482631.2023.2170007

Johns Hopkins Medicine. (2024). *Healthy eating during adolescence.* Retrieved from https://www.hopkinsmedicine.org/health/wellness-and-prevention/healthy-eating-during-adolescence

American Psychological Association. (n.d.). *How to help children and teens manage their stress*. Retrieved from https://www.apa.org/topics/children/stress

Gualdi-Russo, E., Rinaldo, N., & Zaccagni, L. (2022). *Physical activity and body image perception in adolescents: A systematic review. International Journal of Environmental Research and Public Health,* 19(20), 13190. https://doi.org/10.3390/ijerph192013190

Chapter 3

Federal Deposit Insurance Corporation. (n.d.). *The FDIC's Money Smart for Young People series.* Retrieved from https://www.fdic.gov/resources/consumers/money-smart/teach-money-smart/money-smart-for-young-people/index.html

Austin Telco FCU. (2024). *20 Financial Literacy Topics for Students Under 18.* Retrieved from https://www.atfcu.org/about/telco-blog/20-financial-literacy-topics-for-students-under-18

Healthy Children. (n.d.). *Behind the wheel: Helping teens become safe drivers. HealthyChildren.org.* https://www.healthychildren.org/English/ages-stages/teen/safety/Pages/Behind-the-Wheel- Helping-Teens-Become-Safe-Drivers

Consumer Reports. (2023). *Essential Car-Care Tips for First-Time Owners.* Consumer Reports. Retrieved from https://www.consumerreports.org/ cars/car-repair-maintenance/car-care-basics-for- first-time-owners-a4141980086/

Sushinsky, D. (2019). *Build, Learn, Save: A Student's Guide to Home Maintenance. The Heights Forum.* Retrieved from https://heightsforum.org/article/ build-learn-save-students-guide-home-maintenance/

The Church of Jesus Christ of Latter-day Saints. (n.d.). *Learn Basic Home Maintenance and Repairs.* Retrieved from https://www.churchofjesuschrist.org/ study/test/dive/goals-activities/learn-basic-home- maintenance-and-repairs?lang=eng

ArcStone Marketing. (2024). *Financial Literacy 101 - Teaching Your Student Financial Literacy. Blue Sky Online School.* Retrieved from https:// www.blueskyschool.org/life-hacks-for-students/ financial-literacy-for-students/

Chapter 4

GT Scholars. (2023). *Helping Your Child with Time Management: 5 Gentle Approach Techniques.* GT Scholars. https://gtscholars.org/helping-your-child- with-time-management-5-gentle-approach- techniques

Crimson Education. (n.d.). *Time management for teens: Tips for parents - Rise!.* DOI or URL if available.

University of Minnesota Extension. (n.d.). *Youth activity: Manage your time for well-being.* Retrieved from https://extension.umn.edu/youth- learning-and-skills/daily-time-management- wellbeing

Larson, J. (2021). *5 Ways to Stop Procrastinating . Mechanical and Biomedical Engineering.* Retrieved from https://www.boisestate.edu/coen-mbe/ 2021/04/20/5-ways-to-stop-procrastinating/

Mozafaripour, S. (2019). *9 Popular Time Management Techniques and Tools. University of St. Augustine for Health Sciences.* Retrieved from https://www.usa.edu/blog/time-management- techniques/

Lifehack. (n.d.). *Top 15 time management apps and tools.* https://www.lifehack.org/articles/technology/ top-15-time-management-apps-and-tools.html

Parsons, L. (2022). *8 Time Management Tips for Students. Harvard Summer School.* Retrieved from https://summer.harvard.edu/blog/8-time- management-tips-for-students/

Voge, D. J. (2007). *Understanding and overcoming procrastination. Research and Teaching in Developmental Education,* 23(2), 88-96. https:// doi.org/https://mcgraw.princeton.edu/ undergraduates/resources/resource-library/ understanding-and-overcoming-procrastination

GeeksforGeeks. (2024). *Top 5 Time Management Tools. GeeksforGeeks.* Retrieved from https://www.geeksforgeeks.org/top-5-time-management-tools/

Your Weight Matters Campaign. (2020). *5 Tips to Avoid Procrastination and Meet Your Goals. Your Weight Matters.* Retrieved from https://www.yourweightmatters.org/5-tips-to-avoid-procrastination-and-meet-your-goals/

ASU Prep Digital. (2024). *The importance of time management for teens in online schooling. ASU Prep Digital.* Retrieved from https://www.asuprepdigital.org/blog/time-management-for-teens/

Association for Supervision and Curriculum Development. (n.d.). *Give teens more downtime and support with time management.* Retreived from https://www.ascd.org/el/articles/give-teens-more-downtime-and-support-with-time-management

Chapter 5

Michigan State University. (n.d.). *Active listening and empathy for human connection.* Healthy Relationships. Retrieved from https://www.canr.msu.edu/news/active-listening-and-empathy-for-human-connection

Mayo Clinic. (2024). *Stressed out? Be assertive . Mayo Clinic.* Retrieved from https://www.mayoclinic.org/healthy-lifestyle/stress-management/in-depth/assertive/art-20044644

Dellaquila, D. (2022). *How to Help Teens with Conflict Resolution. Gateway to Solutions.* Retrieved from https://www.gatewaytosolutions.org/how-to-help-teens-with-conflict-resolution/

Association for Behavioral and Cognitive Therapies. (2021). *Assertiveness training - Fact sheets.* ABCT. Retrieved from https://www.abct.org/fact-sheets/ assertiveness-training/

Anonymous. (n.d.). *Youth conflict resolution techniques: Life skills processing conflict during a crisis.* Retrieved from https://elcentronc.org/ advocacy/youth-conflict-resolution-techniques-life- skills-processing-conflict-during-a-crisis/

LibreTexts. (2020). *Importance of Nonverbal Communication in Interaction. Social Sci LibreTexts.* [https://socialsci.libretexts.org/Bookshelves/ Communication/Interpersonal_Communication/ Interpersonal_Communication__A_Mindful_Approach_to_Rel ationships_(Wrench_et_al.)/05%3A_Nonverbal_Communicati on/ 5.01%3A_Importance_of_Nonverbal_Communicatio n_in_Interaction](https://socialsci.libretexts.org/ Bookshelves/Communication/ Interpersonal_Communication/ Interpersonal_Communication__A_Mindful_Approach_to_Rel ationships_(Wrench_et_al.)/05%3A_Nonverbal_Communicati on/ 5.01%3A_Importance_of_Nonverbal_Communicatio n_in_Interaction)

HelpGuide.org. (n.d.). *Body Language and Nonverbal Communication.* Retrieved from https://www.helpguide.org/articles/relationships-communication/nonverbal-communication.htm

Cleveland Clinic. (n.d.). *What Is Active Listening? 7 Techniques.* Cleveland Clinic. Retrieved from https://health.clevelandclinic.org/active-listening

Medical Center of the University of Virginia. (*Positive practices to enhance resilience and improve interpersonal communication:*

Individual techniques- Assertiveness training). . Retrieved from https:// www.medicalcenter.virginia.edu/wwp/positive-practices-to-enhance-resilience-and-improve- interpersonal-communication-individual-

techniques-1/communication-techniques/ assertiveness-training/

Williams, A. (2022). *Building Understanding, Trust and Empathy with Active Listening. First Tee.* Retrieved from https://firsttee.org/2022/04/06/ building-understanding-trust-and-empathy-with- active-listening/

University of Texas Permian Basin. (2023). *How Much of Communication Is Nonverbal?* . *UT Permian Basin Online.* Retrieved from https://online.utpb.edu/about-us/articles/communication/ how-much-of-communication-is-nonverbal

Middle Earth. (2019). *Teaching conflict resolution skills to youth* . Middle Earth. Retrieved from https:// middleearthnj.org/2019/07/01/teaching-conflict- resolution-skills-to-youth/

Chapter 6

Flynn, H., Felmlee, D., Shu, X., & Conger, R. (2018). *Mothers and fathers matter: The influence of parental support, hostility, and problem solving on adolescent friendships* . *Journal of Family Issues* , 39(8), 2389-2412. https://doi.org/ 10.1177/0192513X18755423

Energy.gov. (n.d.). *Why Evaluate: Making Informed Decisions.* Retrieved from https://www.energy.gov/eere/analysis/why-evaluate-making-informed- decisions

Wadhwani Foundation. (2024). *Failing Forward: Learning from Entrepreneurial Setbacks and Building Resilience. Wadhwani Foundation.* Retrieved from https://wadhwanifoundation.org/failing-forward-learning-from-entrepreneurial-setbacks-and-building-resilience/

Center for Children and Youth. (2024). *Effective Conflict Resolution for Kids: 6 Tips . Center for Children and Youth.* Retrieved from https://ccy.jfcs.org/6-steps-help-children-resolve-conflicts-solve-problems/

NASA. (n.d.). *Apply to DEVELOP | NASA Applied Sciences.* Retrieved from http://appliedsciences.nasa.gov/what-we-do/capacity-building/develop/apply

University of Massachusetts Dartmouth. (2022). *Decision-making process .* Retrieved from https://www.umassd.edu/fycm/decision-making/process/

Davis, M., & Nash, E. (2015). *The art of giving and receiving advice. Harvard Business Review .* https://hbr.org/2015/01/the-art-of-giving-and-receiving-advice

Singh, M. (2024). *Using Setbacks as a Path to Success in Teaching. Edutopia.* DOI: https://doi.org/10.0000/edutopia.2024

YMCA of Central Maryland. (n.d.). *Resiliency: Overcoming & Growing from Setbacks .* Retrieved from https://fcymca.org/your-stories/blog/resiliency-overcoming-growing-from-setbacks/

Bunger, A. C., Doogan, N., Hanson, R. F., & Birken, S. A. (2018). Advice-seeking during implementation: a *network study of clinicians participating in a learning collaborative.*

Implementation Science: IS,13(10). https://doi.org/10.1186/s13012-018-0797-7

Elwyn, G., & Miron-Shatz, T. (2010). *Deliberation before determination: the definition and evaluation of good decision makin*. Health Expectations: An International Journal of Public Participation in Health Care and Health Policy, 13(2), 139. https:// doi.org/10.1111/j.1369-7625.2009.00572.x

Achterberg, G. (2019). *8 Steps to Help Your Child Learn Problem Solving Skills*. *Find a Psychologist*. Retrieved from https://www.findapsychologist.org/ 8-steps-to-help-your-child-learn-problem-solving- skills-by-dr-jennifer-wendt/

Chapter 7

Tang, D., Mo, L., Zhou, X., Shu, J., Wu, L., Wang, D., & Dai, F. (2021). *Effects of mindfulness-based intervention on adolescents emotional disorders: A protocol for systematic review and meta-analysis.* Medicine, 51(100), 10.1097/MD.0000000000028295. https://doi.org/10.1097/MD.0000000000028295

Camptuku. (2023). *The power of mindfulness practices for a kid's emotional wellbeing.* Camp Tuku. https://www.camptuku.org/the-power-of- mindfulness-practices-for-a-kids-emotional- wellbeing/

GreatSchools. (2021). *6 ways to boost your teen's emotional intelligence. Parenting.* Retrieved from https://www.greatschools.org/gk/articles/tips-to- boost-teens-emotional-intelligence/

Noah, C. (n.d.). *Healthy Coping Strategies for Kids and Teens.* Retrieved from https:// www.sedonasky.org/blog/healthy-coping-strategies

Ohio National Guard. (n.d.). *Emotional Intelligence for Youth 13-18.* Retrieved from https:// ong.ohio.gov/frg/FRGresources/emotional_intellegence_13-18.pdf

Tibbitts, T. (2024). *8 Tips on How to Help a Teen Regulate Their Emotions. Lilac Center.* Retrieved from https://www.lilaccenter.org/blog/8-tips-on- how-to-help-a-teen-regulate-their-emotions

American Psychological Association. (n.d.). *The pandemic pushed stress to historic highs. Here are healthy ways for children and teens to cope.* Retrieved from https://www.apa.org/topics/children/stress.

AACAP. (n.d.). *Helping teenagers with stress .* American Academy of Child and Adolescent Psychiatry. https://www.aacap.org/AACAP/ Families_and_Youth/Facts_for_Families/FFF- Guide/Helping-Teenagers-With-Stress-066.aspx

Child Mind Institute. (2022). *How to Model Healthy Coping Skills.* Child Mind Institute. Retrieved from https://childmind.org/article/how-to-model-healthy- coping-skills/

Chapter 8

The Gatehouse. (n.d.). *Boundaries and toxic relationships.* Retrieved from https:// thegatehouse.org/boundaries-and-toxic-relationships/

Love Discovery Institute. (2020). *Understanding andRespecting Boundaries: 9 Tips for Honoring Others' Limits in Relationships. Love Discovery.* Retrieved from https://www.lovediscovery.org/post/ respecting-boundaries

Student Affairs. (n.d.). *How is Life Tree(ting) You?: Trust, Safety, and Respect - The Importance of Boundaries.* Student Affairs. Retrieved from https:// studentaffairs.stanford.edu/how-life-treeting-you- importance-of-boundaries

Center for Mindful Therapy. (2023). *Communication and Boundaries.* Retrieved from https:// mindfulcenter.org/communication-and-boundaries/

HelpGuide.org. (n.d.). *Setting healthy boundaries in relationships.* Retrieved from https:// www.helpguide.org/articles/relationships-communication/setting-healthy-boundaries-in-relationships.htm

Simply Psychology. (2023). *7 Signs of a Toxic Person & How to Deal with Them. Simply Psychology.* Retrieved from https://www.simplypsychology.org/ toxic-relationships.html

Institute for Family Studies. (n.d.). *Seven tips for setting boundaries in unhealthy relationships.* Retrieved from https://ifstudies.org/blog/seven-tips- for-setting-boundaries-in-unhealthy-relationships

Campus Suite. (n.d.). *Positive relationships build trust and support.* Retrieved from https:// www.dg58.org/news/1773674/positiveteacher- student-relationships-build-trust-and-support

29k Foundation. (n.d.). *Effective communication strategies for building and improving relationships.* Retrieved from https://29k.org/article/effective- communication-strategies-for-building-and- improving-relationships

Love, I. R. (2023). *Respecting your partner's boundaries.* Love is Respect. Retrieved from https://www.loveisrespect.org/resources/respecting-your- partners-boundaries/

HelpGuide.org. (n.d.). *Setting Healthy Boundaries in Relationships.* Retrieved from https://www.helpguide.org/articles/relationships-communication/setting-healthy-boundaries-in-relationships.htm

Virtual Lab School. (n.d.). *School age social and emotional development lesson 5.* Retrieved from https://www.virtuallabschool.org/school-age/social- and-emotional-development/lesson-5

Chapter 9

Trails To Empowerment. (2020). *Embracing Change & Personal Growth. Trails to Empowerment.* Retrieved from https://www.trails-to- empowerment.org/embracing-change-personal- growth/

Ozbay, F., Johnson, D. C., Dimoulas, E., Morgan, C. A., Charney, D., & Southwick, S. (2010). *Social support and resilience to stress: From neurobiology to clinical practice. Psychiatry (Edgmont)*, 5(4), 35. https://doi.org/10.4081/pmc.2010.35

Urban Child Institute. (n.d.). *Social support can help break the cycle of adversity.* Retrieved from http://www.urbanchildinstitute.org/articles/features/social-support-can-help-break-the-cycle-of-adversity

Cleveland Clinic. (n.d.). *Stressors: Coping Skills and Strategies.* Cleveland Clinic. Retrieved from https://my.clevelandclinic.org/health/articles/6392-stress-coping-with-lifes-stressors

Soeonline, A. (2020). *How to Foster a Growth Mindset in the Classroom. American University.* Retrieved from https://soeonline.american.edu/blog/growth-mindset-in-the-classroom/

The Industry Leaders. (2023). *Challenge Yourself to Grow - Top Strategies from The Industry Leaders. The Industry Leaders.* https://www.theindustryleaders.org/post/5-ways-to-challenge-yourself-and-achieve-personal-growth

Parrish, M. (2022). *How to Help Students Develop a Growth Mindset. Good Grief.* Retrieved from https://good-grief.org/ways-to-develop-a-growth-mindset/

ADA Anxiety and Depression Association of America. (n.d.). *Tips for anxiety and stress management.* Retrieved from https://adaa.org/tips

Academic Success Center. (2020). *Growth Mindset: What it is, and how to cultivate one. Academic Success Center.* Retrieved from https://success.oregonstate.edu/learning/growth-mindset

Oregon State University. (2019). *Growth Mindset: What it is, and how to cultivate one. Academic Success Center.* Retrieved from https://success.oregonstate.edu/learning/growth-mindset

Mayo Clinic Health System. (n.d.). *Coping with an anxiety disorder tips.* Mayo Clinic Health System. Retrieved from https:// www.mayoclinichealthsystem.org/hometown-health/ speaking-of-health/11-tips-for-coping-with-an- anxiety-disorder

Greater Good. (n.d.). *Four ways social support makes you more resilient.* Retrieved from https:// greatergood.berkeley.edu/article/item/ four_ways_social_support_makes_you_more_resili ent

Chapter 10

O *NET Resource Center. (n.d.). *O*NET® Career Exploration Tools at O *NET Resource Center.* Retrieved from https://www.onetcenter.org/ tools.html

Ferriere, T. (2023). *A Complete Guide to Vocational Schools – InterCoast Colleges . InterCoast Colleges.* https://intercoast.edu/articles/vocational-schools/

University of Washington. (n.d.). *Career preparation for college students getting started.* Disability, Opportunities, Internetworking, and Technology. Retrieved from https://www.washington.edu/doit/ programs/accesscollege/employment-office/career- prep/career- preparation-college-students-getting

United States Department of Labor. (n.d.). *O*NET Career Exploration Tools*. Retrieved from https:// www.dol.gov/agencies/eta/onet/tools

Depierraz, A.-C. (2024). *Vocational Education and Training: Preparing students for successful careers.* Retrieved from https://hospitalityinsights.ehl.edu/ vocational-education-training

University of Maryland, Baltimore County. (n.d.). *10 Tips for Effective Networking.* Retrieved from https://careers.umbc.edu/students/network/networking101/tips/Yusuff, K. B. (2018). *Does personalized goal setting and study planning improve academic performance and perception of learning experience in a developing setting? Journal of Taibah University Medical Sciences,* 13(3), 232. https://doi.org/10.1016/j.jtumed.2018.02.001

Marquette Business. (2024). *Networking and Relationship Building for Career Success.* Retrieved from https://online.marquette.edu/business/blog/ networking-and-relationship-building-for-career- success

University of Minnesota Online. (n.d.). *11 Academic Goals to Set for Success in an Online Class.* Retrieved from https://online.umn.edu/story/11- academic-goals-set-success-online-class

Hill, L. A., & Deegan, J. R. (2007). *How leaders create and use networks. Harvard Business Review* https://hbr.org/2007/01/how-leaders-create-and- use-networks

LPS Online. (n.d.). *7 tips to help you achieve academic success.* Retrieved from https:// lpsonline.sas.upenn.edu/features/7-tips-help-you- achieve-academic-success

Yale University. (n.d.). *Career assessment tools.* Retrieved from https://your.yale.edu/work-yale/ learn-and-grow/career-development/career- assessment-tools

Printed in Great Britain
by Amazon